A SHORT
HISTORY
OF THE
CAMERA

A SHORT HISTORY OF THE CAMERA

BY JOHN WADE

FOUNTAIN PRESS

FOUNTAIN PRESS
Argus Books Limited
14 St James Road
Watford, Hertfordshire.

ISBN 0 85242 640 2
First published 1979

Printed and bound in England by G. A. Pindar & Son Ltd.
Scarborough, N. Yorkshire.

Typeset in Garamond by The Humble Wordsmith Limited
187 High Street, Tonbridge, Kent

Contents

1

Things that go black in the light

The difficulty is knowing where to start. We could begin perhaps with Daguerre, for it was he who gave us the first practical method of making pictures, and the original Daguerreotype Camera of 1839 was a very sophisticated instrument for its day. Indeed, within hours of the daguerreotype process being announced, the manufacturers were swamped with orders; so it could be considered as the earliest commercially successful camera. But it was by no means the first.

The first camera actually used for making a picture must go back to 1826, the year Niépce used it to produce what has come to be accepted as the first photograph. Yet even this wasn't really the first camera. The first *photographic* camera maybe, but the fact of the matter is that cameras were invented a long time before photography and what we are talking about now is the camera obscura, a device that can be traced back as far as the 11th Century.

These original camera obscuras were vastly different from the cameras they were later to become. For a start, you couldn't have held one in your hand; you would have had to stand inside it. They started as darkened rooms with one small hole in a wall projecting an image of the scene outside onto the opposite wall in much the same way as a pin-hole camera projects an object onto film. The only use for the camera obscuras in these early days seems to have been for observing the sun.

In 1550, Girolamo Cardano, a physician and professor of mathematics, announced that if a biconvex lens was used rather than a bare, empty hole in the wall, a far brighter and sharper image could be achieved. The idea was enthusiastically taken up by writer and scientist Giovanni Battista della Porta, who began experimenting with various lenses until he obtained the best and sharpest image possible. Then he invited an audience to watch as a group of hired actors outside the room were projected onto the wall inside.

The reaction of what could possibly be described as the first cinema audience was not too good. The sight of the actors, ghost-like and upside-down, moving as if by magic on the wall proved too much for them. They panicked and della Porta was subsequently charged with sorcery.

But by the 17th Century camera obscuras had been promoted from the realms of magic to become accepted as genuine scientific instruments much favoured by artists as an aid to sketching. They soon became portable — in so far as a decent sized room could be said to be portable. One such model took the form of two collapsible rooms, one inside the other. The user stood inside the smaller room and viewed the scene around him back-projected through the outer wall, onto the inner wall.

Towards the end of the Century and into the early 1700s, the portable camera obscura took on many weird and wonderful forms. Some were cone-shaped, others were square, but there was always a lens at one end to project the image onto a screen at the other, together with some contrivance that necessitated the artist enclosing his entire head and drawing arm in the dark behind the screen — the only way he could actually see the image in daylight.

There were camera obscuras designed in the form of tables for interior work and others built into tents for outside. There were even models designed as sedan chairs. They were, however, camera obscuras straight and simple, used by artists and destined to have little or no bearing on future photographic apparatus.

The image of leaves recorded on sensitized paper. A modern equivalent of the photographic experiments of Thomas Wedgwood.

To see the point where the camera obscura first began to resemble a photographic camera, we must go back to 1676, to a point when the instrument's history came to a fork. One road led to sedan chairs and the like, the other contained Johann Christoph Sturm.

Sturm was a professor of mathematics at Altdorf University who described and illustrated the first reflex camera obscura. For the first time, a model was designed with a mirror at 45 degrees to the lens which reflected the image right way up onto a piece of oiled paper stretched across an opening in the camera top. This viewing screen was shaded by a box-like arrangement made of paper, into which the artist could insert both his hand and his head. It was a decided improvement on the room within a room arrangement, but its portability was still somewhat suspect.

Then, nine years later, the German monk, Johann Zahn designed a model small enough to be carried anywhere, that to all intents and purposes was a single lens reflex. It

A tent form of camera obscura made by Chevalier in the early 1800s.

measured 60cms long by 22.5cms high, the lens was mounted in an adjustable tube that focused the image via a 45 degree mirror onto opal glass, flaps on the lid shielded the viewing screen and the inside was painted black to kill unwanted reflections.

For the first time in the history of the camera, there was an instrument that could be carried easily from place to place and which was theoretically capable of taking a photograph. The year was 1685 — nearly 150 years before such a thing would prove possible.

The camera owes its existence to an equal marriage of physics and chemistry, the former providing the optical and mechanical side, the latter looking after the light-sensitive materials that make photography possible; and while the physics was now ready, the chemistry still had a long way to go. Not that scientists of the time were entirely ignorant about light-sensitive chemicals. Many were aware that silver nitrate turned black when exposed to the sun; unfortunately they attributed this not to the sun's light, but to its heat.

The first man to prove that certain compounds of silver were light-sensitive rather than heat-sensitive was Johann Heinrich Schulze. He was a professor of anatomy and, purely by accident while trying to make phosphorus, he discovered that a flask filled with nitric acid and a little silver, mixed with some chalk, turned from white to a deep purple when exposed to sunlight.

The picture that started it all. The courtyard as seen from Niépce's attic window. The picture, on a pewter plate, is the earliest photograph in existence today.

10

He made stencils of words and even complete sentences which he taped to the side of his flask before exposing it to light. The result was dark words against a white background. With no way of fixing the image, however, it wasn't long before his silhouettes disappeared as the entire mixture darkened in the light.

That was in 1725 and over the next few years, a number of men became involved with photochemistry. Silver nitrate was firmly established as a light-sensitive chemical, silver chloride was also discovered to have similar properties and there followed experiments with the chemicals in both liquid form and as a coating on paper.

Towards the end of the 18th Century Thomas Wedgwood, son of the famous potter, began experimenting with sensitized paper. He made white against black copies of insects' wings and leaves by simply laying them on the paper and exposing it to light. He also managed, by the same method, to copy pictures that had been painted on glass. There was, however, no way to fix the images he obtained and they could be viewed only by candle light.

Undeterred by this quite serious drawback, Wedgwood next took his experiments one last and remarkably relevant step forward. He put a sheet of sensitized paper into a camera obscura, convinced that he would be able to capture its image. It was 1802 and photography was a hairsbreadth from discovery. But it was not to be. Wedgwood failed, probably through too little exposure of the material. Had he left his paper in the camera obscura longer, he would undoubtably have obtained an image and might now be credited as the inventor of photography.

As it was, he became convinced after too short a time that the process was impractical and gave up that particular line of research. Fourteen years later, the idea was turned into a practical proposition by the son of a King's Counsellor in France. His name was Joseph Nicéphore Niépce.

Right from childhood, Niépce had been a born inventor, always on the look-out for something new with which to experiment. Together with his brother Claude, he invented a hot air engine and even produced an early type of bicycle. In 1816, he began experimenting with camera obscuras, trying to record the scene from his attic window using paper sensitized with silver chloride.

At this time, he was using a locally made camera about 15 cm square with an adjustable tube supporting the lens. He also had a tiny camera made from a jewel box, fitted with a microscope lens, giving an image under 3 cm square and a slightly larger one fitted with a similar lens. It was with one of these that Niépce actually succeeded in producing the world's first negative which he partially fixed with nitric acid.

It was a few years later, in 1819, that the celebrated English astronomer Sir John Herschel discovered the way sodium thiosulphate (which he mistakenly called hyposulphite of soda) dissolved various silver compounds and, had Niépce known of this discovery, he might have used the knowledge to permanently fix his first negatives. As it was, he abandoned the idea in favour of a different and far less practical method of recording images.

(It is interesting to note here that the man who is generally credited as producing the world's first negative is Henry Talbot. The credit is rightly attributed since it was he who first saw the practical implications of the negative as it is used in today's negative-positive system. And yet, Talbot's famous 'first negative' of the lattice window at Lacock Abbey in England was made some nineteen years after Niépce produced his negatives in France.)

The reason Niépce shied away from the negative image was quite simply because it *was* a negative. He was after a method of recording accurate pictures of scenes from nature and black skies with white shadows didn't answer his needs. He wanted positives, not negatives. To give credit where it is due, it must be said that he did try making positives by contact printing his negatives with fresh sheets of sensitized paper, but to no avail. The results didn't satisfy him and so he began looking in other directions to find what must have seemed the obvious aim at the time — a method of producing a positive first time in the camera.

The light dawned in 1826 and came from his interest in lithography. Earlier experiments in this field had led Niépce to a knowledge of bitumen of Judea, a kind of asphalt whose most important properties in this context were these: it hardened when exposed to light, the hardened bitumen was pale white in colour, the unexposed material remained soft and could be dissolved in lavender oil.

Dissolving the bitumen of Judea in lavender oil, Niépce coated a glass plate with the mixture. A line drawing, made translucent with oil was placed face down on the glass and then exposed to the sun.

Where the light shone through the blank areas of the drawing, the bitumen of Judea hardened. Where the dark lines of the drawing shielded the sun's rays, it remained soft and therefore soluble. It could then be washed away with more lavender oil and a positive image was thus left behind. What was more, it was permanent. It couldn't fade because the sensitive soft bitumen had been washed away.

From there, it was only a short and very logical step for Niépce to try the process out in a camera obscura. Evidence points to the fact that he used his first professionally made model for the purpose, built for him by Charles and Vincent Chevalier, the famous Paris opticians, and fitted with a prism to correct the picture which would have been laterally reversed in the normal way.

For the previous few years, Niépce had been experimenting with various bases for his process and by now, having tried glass, copper and zinc, he had eventually settled on pewter. So a pewter plate was coated in bitumen of Judea, fitted into the back of his camera and placed on a window-sill with the lens aimed at the courtyard outside. It was left there all day.

At the end of the day, Niépce removed the plate. The bitumen had hardened and turned white where the light had fallen. He dissolved the remaining soft bitumen with lavender oil, leaving the pale hardened substance to portray the highlights while the base metal, darkened by treatment with iodine vapour, showed the shadows.

The process was totally impractical and the exposure time nothing short of ludicrous; but whatever failings the system had, one thing was for sure. Joseph Nicéphore Niépce had just taken the first fully-fixed, positive picture. He called the process heliographie. The year was 1826. And the history of the camera as we know it today had begun.

2

From today painting is dead

A daguerreotype of Mme Daguerre, taken by her husband.

Between 1826 and his death seven years later, Niépce used several cameras still in existence which were way ahead of their time. We have already mentioned the one made by the Chevaliers on which the first photograph was almost certainly taken and it was this firm who made what is now reckoned to be the earliest known camera still surviving.

This was designed on the sliding box principle; two boxes, one which slid within the other to give the degree of movement necessary for focusing. The camera measured 30.5 x 31.5 x 38.5 cm with a format of 16 x 19 cm. The lens, no longer in existence, is thought to have been biconvex with a focal length of 300mm.

The sliding box design was one that would dominate cameras for many years to come, but Niépce also owned a crude form of bellows camera. The biggest single problem of his process was the overlong exposure times, and yet Niépce used another camera that utilized a variable iris diaphragm — not to lengthen the exposure time even more, but because he discovered that a smaller aperture would sharpen the image. Many of his cameras also had small holes in one side with a plug that could be removed for the user to observe the image as it slowly appeared on the plate.

There is no doubt at all that Niépce was a great innovator, but as far as progress was concerned, heliographie was a dead end. There was no way of improving it, nowhere for it to go; and so it fell to someone else to come up with a different process which, in its way, proved to be just as much of a dead end, but unlike heliographie, was at least practical. The process, which caught the imagination of an entire generation, was the daguerreotype process; the inventor was Louis Jacques Mandé Daguerre.

Daguerre came to hear of Niépce's work through the Chevaliers who made camera obscuras for both men. When he heard that Niépce had actually managed to permanently record the instrument's image, he became intrigued because he had, for some time, been trying to do the same thing. He immediately wrote to Niépce and suggested a

The original Daguerreotype Camera of 1839.

meeting. For a while, Niépce remained suspicious of this total stranger who had approached him out of the blue, but after making some inquiries about the man, he eventually agreed to meet Daguerre. He found a man whose energy was surpassed only by his versatility.

Daguerre was a keen and talented artist, a fact that had led to his apprenticeship as an architect. From there, he went on to become a scenery painter with the Paris Opera, progressing after a while to designing theatrical scenery. The theatre would seem to have worked its way into his blood because he was also a ballet dancer and acrobat with a talent for tight-rope walking.

Scientifically, he had no qualifications at all. What he did have was tremendous drive and unbounded enthusiam for whatever subject caught his imagination. Diorama was a typical example.

By painting pictures and parts of pictures on a number of translucent screens arranged one behind the other, Diorama created three-dimensional illusions by the use of clever lighting. Audiences could sit in the specially built halls and watch as church interiors or exterior landscape

15

views appeared and vanished before their startled eyes, complete with music and sound effects.

It was like magic and one of its inventors was Daguerre. With such a background, it isn't surprising that the man eventually turned his interest and remarkably talented mind to the subject of cameras.

Despite their widely different backgrounds, Niépce and Daguerre became friends and partners. The partnership was formed initially to perfect and improve heliographie and over the next four years, they each worked separately, reporting their experiments to one another by mail. But no improvements were forthcoming and all Daguerre actually added to the partnership was better camera obscuras.

It wasn't until after Niépce's death that Daguerre finally came up with his own process which, while owing much to his ex-partner's knowledge, was vastly different from heliographie — a fact that Daguerre felt justified calling it by a different name. And so the daguerreotype was born.

The biggest one factor that contributed to its success was Daguerre's discovery of the latent image; discovered, in fact, by accident when he left an underexposed plate in a cupboard with a broken thermometer and returned to find an image had appeared as a result of the mercury fumes.

The first daguerreotypes were made in 1835, but it wasn't until 1837 that Daguerre found a way of fixing them, using a solution of common salt. Briefly then, this is how the process worked:-

A plate of copper, coated with silver, was cleaned and polished to spotless perfection, using pumice and olive oil. A high gloss on the plate was essential to the process. Now, by the light of nothing brighter than a candle, the plate was exposed to iodine crystals. This would have been in an airtight box as fumes from iodine were particularly dangerous. The fumes combined with the silver on the plate to form silver iodide, a light-sensitive compound.

When the plate had taken on a golden-yellow colour, it was ready for exposure. The subject in these early days was likely to have been a building, a landscape or still life as exposure times, even in strong sunlight, were still in the region of fifteen minutes, making portraiture impractical. During the exposure, the silver iodide was reduced to silver by the action of light.

Developing was as dangerous as sensitizing. In the latter, the photographer ran the risk of exposure to iodine fumes; in developing, he stood the chance of finding himself exposed to mercury fumes.

The mercury was heated in a dish over a lamp, the whole set-up inside an air-tight box. The exposed plate was now slotted face down into the box so that the fumes could rise from the heated mercury and react with the silver to form a white amalgam. Development was by inspection, through a window in the box, watching the image on the plate reflected in the pool of mercury beneath.

The plate was then removed from the box. The white amalgam made up the highlights of the picture and the salt solution was used to wash away the unaffected silver iodide so that the shadows were represented by the unchanged, polished silver beneath. Later, when Daguerre heard of Herschel's hypo, he used this in place of salt to fix his images.

At that time, Herschel, whose own experiments continually touched on light sensitive materials, was presenting a paper to the Royal Society with the title, 'The Art of Photography, or The Application of the Chemical Rays of Light to the Purpose of Pictorial Representation'. It was the first time the word *photography* had been used officially.

It was used again when Daguerre's process was announced to the French Academy of Sciences in 1839, and such was its success that artists of the time immediately began fearing for their jobs. 'From today, painting is dead,' announced the French painter Paul Delaroche when he was shown his first daguerreotype, and he meant it. For the first time, someone with no artistic ability whatsoever could reproduce scenes from nature with more accuracy than the most proficient of artists.

The daguerreotype process had arrived with a vengeance, but what of the cameras that used it?

The original Daguerreotype Camera of 1839 was designed by Daguerre himself and built by Alphonse Giroux of Paris. It measured 50 x 37 x 31 cm and took 21.5 x 16.5 cm plates, the size which became known as whole plate only when smaller cameras were later built.

The f/17 lens had a focal length of 20.25 cm and focusing was by the sliding box method. Exposure was controlled by a metal cap across the lens that could be slid aside and replaced after the appropriate amount of time; hinged to the back of the camera was a mirror at 45 degrees to correct the image on the ground-glass focusing screen — although it was, of course, still laterally reversed unless a prism was used in front of the lens; and on one side of each camera there was a plaque, signed by Daguerre, guaranteeing success.

While the Giroux camera was perfectly capable of landscape work and was in fact used for such, the first true landscape camera was made by an amateur in the same year of 1839. He was Baron Pierre Armand Seguier and he designed the first daguerreotype bellows camera. Two sets of bellows opened each way from a central fixed point and when folded, the camera could be stored in a large but portable box that contained all the equipment needed for working the complicated process. Even the camera's tripod could be converted into a mobile darkroom by throwing a canvas cover over the top, making a dark tent for the photographer to work in.

The daguerreotype had three main disadvantages. The first of these was in the viewing; depending on the angle at which light struck the surface of the plate, the person looking at the picture might have seen a positive, a negative or even a combination of both.

The second drawback lay in the fact that the daguerreotype was a one-off process; the finished picture was on the actual plate that came out of the camera and therefore could not be duplicated.

The third problem was still the lengthy exposure times that made portraiture impractical. Though this was not a fault of the process, only of the cameras of the time. The f/17 lens of Daguerre's original camera was just not gathering enough light.

It was a problem that was overcome by the insight of an Austrian professor named Andreas Von Ettinghausen, who was present when Daguerre's process was first announced. Even in 1839 he recognised the need for a better lens and, at home in Austria, he rapidly got together with Joseph Petzval, a mathematician and Peter Von Voigtlander, head of the famous optical firm.

By 1840, Petzval had designed a lens with an aperture of f/3.6 which immediately cut exposure times and made portraiture a practical proposition. It was fitted into a camera built by Voigtlander and whose design owed more to the telescope than to any camera so far seen. It was made of brass and consisted of two long cones with a focusing screen in the centre. The front cone supported the lens, the rear cone held a magnifier for inspecting the image on the ground-glass screen and the whole assembly was held in a metal cradle.

The camera was ideally suited to portraiture and yet, when Richard Beard opened the first photographic studio at London's Royal Polytechnic Institution in 1841, he used a daguerreotype camera of even more unusual design and one

Processing equipment needed for the daguerrotype process.

18

that did absolutely nothing to influence future apparatus. The camera, designed by Alexander Woolcott of New York, used a concave mirror in place of a lens. The mirror was positioned at the *back* of the camera and gathered light through an aperture in the front. It reflected its image onto a plate inserted through an opening in the camera's side at the point of the mirror's focus and the sensitized side of the plate was naturally faced *away* from the object or person to be photographed.

Beard was the first of several leading portrait photographers to be approached by Sir Charles Wheatstone with what must have seemed an unusual request. He wanted two pictures of the same subject taken from slightly different positions so that the displacement between the two positions of the lens was approximately that of the human eyes. What Wheatstone wanted in fact was a stereo pair.

The difference between two views of a single object seen by each of the eyes was observed as far back as 280 B.C., but it wasn't until 1832 that Wheatstone found that the appearance of three dimensions could be faked by making a couple of two-dimensional drawings from different viewpoints and then arranging·them in a special viewer so that each eye saw only one of the drawings.

So when photography came along, the theory behind stereo pictures was ready and waiting, although, due to the design of the early viewers which let light in from all directions and the way daguerreotypes relied on the angle of light for their viewing, they didn't prove very successful in the first instance. It wasn't until the more conventional enclosed viewers were later made that daguerreotype stereo pairs became more practical.

Far better for stereo photography was the paper-based calotype picture that arrived soon after the daguerreotype. Of which, more later.

During the 1840s, as the daguerreotype process became more and more popular, different designs of camera began springing up literally all over the world.

In 1840 Charles Chevalier designed and built a collapsible daguerreotype camera with an f/5.6 lens which folded from 28cm in its working position to 9.5cm for carrying; in 1841, Alexis Gaudin of Paris departed from Daguerre's original size plates to produce a model taking pictures 7 x 8cm in a camera with three aperture stops from f/4 to f/24; and in America, John Plumbe made a sliding box camera in 1842 very much like Daguerre's original model but smaller, being only 14.5 x 14.75 x 11.5cm.

The Voigtlander daguerrotype camera which made portraiture practical for the first time.

Like much that had gone before and much more that was still to come, Daguerre's invention was clumsy and, in some respects, a positive danger to health. Its saving grace was quite simply that it *worked* and its biggest attraction was its use for portraiture. In an age when the only previous method had been painting or drawing, a person could now have his likeness reproduced by the far quicker and relatively inexpensive daguerreotype.

Customers flocked to studios from far and wide as the family portrait suddenly ceased to be the prerogative of the rich. Portraiture for the masses had arrived at last.

3

The day of the mousetraps

A reflex camera obscura used by Talbot.

Niépce took the first photograph, Daguerre adapted the process to his own ends and made it far more practical, and yet the man who is probably credited more than any other with being the father of photography is William Henry Fox Talbot.

When the daguerreotype process was made public in 1839, the news must have brought deep disappointment to Talbot. For the previous five years, he had been working to perfect a photographic process of his own and he had every hope of being the first to announce a practical method of photography to the world.

Talbot was a man of extraordinary vision. He was Squire of the Manor in the Wiltshire village of Lacock and his talents took in much more than the early photographic experiments with which he is more usually associated. A brilliant mathematician, researcher into light and optics, the inventor of the polarizing microscope and a finger in every pie from English Literature to astronomy, taking in botany on the way, that was Talbot. He wrote three volumes on etymology, published the first book to be illustrated by photographs and was a Member of Parliament for a few brief years.

Even at the age of seven, his diary showed that he was experimenting with optics and later, at Harrow, he actually caused an explosion which consequently had him banned from active experimentation. After Harrow, he went on to Trinity College, Cambridge, but it was later, in his thirties that his truly creative work began.

During the decade that spanned 1830 to 1840, he flirted for a while with politics, married his wife Constance, became involved in chemical, physical and mathematical research, published the three etymological volumes and finally began his researches into photography.

He had been led to his photographic experiments, like so many before him, by a fascination for the camera obscura and another artist's aid of the day known as a camera lucida. His early experiments were along similar lines to those of

Thomas Wedgwood, producing silhouettes of leaves, lace and feathers on sensitized paper — no developing, just exposing until the image physically appeared. Unlike Wedgwood, however, he found a way of fixing his images with a solution of salt.

This breakthrough came because Talbot coated his paper with silver chloride (common salt) before applying the usual silver nitrate. This gave him a coating of silver chloride which he hoped would be more sensitive than the nitrate compound. In fact, it showed him that the more salt he used, the slower was the speed with which the paper darkened in the light, a fact that led him straight to the use of salt water as a fixing agent.

But negative images, even if they were fixed, were not enough to satisfy Talbot. He soon took his process a step further and in so doing, he made history. Because rather than search for a way of making positives in the camera the way others had, Talbot paved the way for the negative-positive system of today's photography by contact printing his negative picture with a fresh piece of sensitized paper, using the sun as his light source.

The natural and, by now, obvious last stage was to try fixing the image from a camera obscura. His initial experiment failed through lack of adequate exposure, something which he was swift to recognise; but while others had concentrated on building bigger and better lenses, Talbot

Three of Talbot's cameras. Left to right: A wooden box model with ratchet to tilt the camera to any desired angle, another camera made from deal with a curved back to allow for the lens's curvature of field and one of Talbot's earliest cameras used for both photogenic drawing and calotypes. Note the holes and plugs in the lens panels of all three.

William Talbot, inventor of the calotype process.

22

turned in a different direction. He started making smaller cameras.

Small cameras with short focal length lenses meant that the light gathered by the lens could be concentrated on a small area, rather than spread over a large one, resulting in a brighter image and consequently shorter exposure times. The cameras, made by a village carpenter and fitted with microscope lenses, were no more than 6cm square, giving images 2.5cm square. They sat quite comfortably in the palm of the hand, a fact that seems to have endeared them to Talbot's wife, Constance; for it was she who gave them the name that passed into history. Because they were so small, she called them Mousetrap Cameras.

It was with one of these in 1835 that Talbot made the earliest negative still surviving. The picture was one of a lattice window at Lacock Abbey, taken from inside looking out and exposure time was within the region of half an hour.

The process itself, which still relied on the negative material being exposed until an image actually appeared upon it, was known as photogenic drawing and it never really caught on seriously. The latent image, whose discovery would have cut exposure times so drastically was still unknown to Talbot and during the next four years, he concentrated on adapting photogenic drawing to various subjects that ranged from the exteriors of buildings to pictures through a solar microscope.

It wasn't until 1839, when news of Daguerre's process reached his ears that Talbot began trying to speed up his own process. The mousetrap cameras, he realized by now, were defeating their own object. Their image was brighter, the exposure time was less, but with no way of enlarging in those days, who wanted a picture only 2.5cm square?

During 1839, Andrew Ross made some larger cameras for Talbot that were fitted with achromatic lenses and it was while using these that he had a lucky accident that changed the course of his experiments overnight.

Having underexposed some sheets of sensitized paper during the course of one experiment, he put them in a cupboard with the thought of using them again. When the need arose, he took the paper from the cupboard and began resensitizing it. To his astonishment, an image appeared — a picture of the scene that he thought to have been underexposed. And so, like Daguerre before him, Talbot discovered the latent image purely by accident.

It was 1840 and for the first time, with exposures down to as little as three minutes, Talbot had a method of taking

A positive from the earliest surviving negative, made by Talbot with his photogenic drawing method.

portraits. What started as a lucky accident ended as a whole new photographic process whose name was taken by Talbot from the Greek word *kalos*, meaning beautiful. He called his pictures calotypes. This is how they were made:-

Using a candle for illumination, a sheet of good quality writing paper was washed, dried and then sensitized by first floating it in silver nitrate solution. This took about three minutes and the resultant coating was allowed to dry before soaking the paper again in potassium iodide solution. The two chemicals reacted to produce the light-sensitive silver iodide. In this state, the paper could be kept until required.

When a photograph was to be taken, the paper was brushed with a solution of silver nitrate, acetic acid and gallic acid to make it more sensitive, partially dried and used in the camera still damp. The exposure was then made — anything between one and two minutes.

After exposure, the paper was again treated with silver nitrate, acetic acid and gallic acid, then warmed in front of a fire for a few minutes when the image finally appeared. It was fixed, in the early days with potassium bromide, but later, when Talbot learnt of Herschel's discovery, he too used hypo for the purpose.

For printing, silver chloride paper was used, prepared by floating the paper first in ammonium chloride and then in silver nitrate. The paper negative was placed in contact with this, emulsion to emulsion and exposed to the light of the sun until the positive image appeared on the new sheet of paper. It was then fixed in the normal way.

A finished calotype, because of the paper's texture, ended up as a soft-looking print with slightly fuzzy edges. It never did acquire the sharp definition of the daguerreotype but in many ways, especially in portraiture and landscapes, its very imperfections were a major part of its charm.

We've looked at the process, now let's look at the cameras that used it.

We have already mentioned the Mousetrap Cameras and even when Talbot had larger cameras made, the early designs followed the cube-shaped designs. Those used for photogenic drawing had plugs in the lens panels that could

A typical calotype print.

be removed to see how the image was progressing; but later, when Talbot discovered the latent image and exposure times became shorter, his new cameras were built without these spy-holes as they would have admitted too much light and spoilt the picture.

The early cameras had lenses held in adjustable focusing tubes and one had a ratchet that wound the camera to any degree of tilt that the user might require to take his picture. Another of his cameras was made of deal with a back that curved the paper to allow for the lens's curvature of field.

Most of these cameras, however, were really quite crude — no more than a box with some device for altering the distance between lens and sensitive paper. But with the end of photogenic drawing and the beginning of the calotype process, Talbot began looking towards more sophistication in his cameras. He bought a Giroux daguerreotype camera which he adapted for use with calotypes. For portraiture, he used a fixed focus, all metal camera made by Lerebours of Paris. The camera, which had a choice of three apertures on a sliding disc in front of the lens, was in the form of a metal cylinder attached to a square holder for the sensitized paper.

In 1845, the same company made a sliding box camera for calotypes 8 x 9cm. This too had a choice of apertures on a rotating disc and the ground-glass screen was shielded by a folding wooden hood that took the place of the more traditional black cloth.

Talbot also used a 6.5 x 7.5 cm camera fitted with a special lens made by Chevalier and which was supplied with two different front elements — one for landscapes, the other for portraiture.

Yet despite the fact that photographic processes were changing and improving all the time, the 1840s were surprisingly devoid of any real revolution in camera design. Most of the cameras used by Talbot and his contemporaries were no more than adaptations or slight improvements on those used by Niépce thirty years before. One of the few exceptions was the brainchild of an amateur named George Cundell.

Cundell's calotype camera of 1844 was designed on the sliding box principle without a baseboard, just two boxes, one which slid within the other. It boasted three firsts: a focusing scale, a lens hood and internal baffles to cut down reflections inside the camera. The focusing scale, however, was there for more than the expected reason. The camera was fitted with a simple meniscus lens that was prone to all the aberrations of its type, not the least of which was the fact

'Pencil of Nature'. The first book to be photographically illustrated.

that rays from the violet end of the spectrum came to a point of focus before those from the red end. And, as it was the violet rays that had most effect on the photographic emulsions of those days, it was possible for an image that appeared sharp as a pin on the focusing screen to be just off focus on the negative.

Cundell got round this problem by fitting his camera with not one focusing scale, but two. The image was focused on the ground-glass screen, a number was read off on the first scale and then focus shifted so that the corresponding number was now adjusted on the second scale. The result was a perfectly focused picture every time.

It wasn't until the 1850s, that camera manufacturers began getting more adventurous with their designs and then they turned their thoughts towards making models with the accent on convenience. Lighter cameras, models that were easy to carry around became the order of the day.

An early form of magazine camera made its appearance in 1850, designed by Marcus Sparling. In this, ten sheets of paper could be stored in separate holders ready for use and, after exposure, each sheet dropped down into a compartment under the camera.

In 1851, Richard Willats came up with a design whose body was made, not of wood or metal, but of cloth. The camera back could be clamped onto a sliding plate in the base and was separated from the lens panel by the conical-shaped cloth body that expanded and contracted as necessary so that lenses of various focal lengths could be used. The result was a camera that took pictures as large as 26.5 x 22 cm but collapsed to only 10 cm deep when folded.

In 1853, there was another magazine camera devised by George Stokes which could take up to twenty calotypes in rapid succession; but one of the most ingenious devices of the decade came from A. J. Melhuish and J. B. Spencer who, in 1854, dreamt up what must surely have been the first spool of roll film. It was made up of sensitized wax paper, rolled onto spools of different sizes and fitted into a special holder that could be fitted to the back of a camera.

But we're getting beyond ourselves. Back in the 1840s, if *cameras* weren't so inventive, *processes* were. Although Talbot is the man most associated with paper negatives, it must be noted before leaving the era that he was by no means the only scientist in the field. From the moment a practical method of photography was first announced, experimentors everywhere began jumping on the bandwagon.

Dedicated scientists, out and out amateurs, everyone from vets (Friedrich Gerber) to clergymen (The Rev. J. B. Reade) started claiming and showing proof of prints on paper and even some on leather. Sir John Herschel, within a week of hearing about Daguerre's success, succeeded in making a picture on paper sensitized with silver carbonate and, of course, fixed with hypo — his own discovery.

One of the most significant advances was made by a French civil servant named Hippolyte Bayard whose process, if it had been given better recognition, could have been a strong rival for the daguerreotype. In 1839, he made photogenic drawings similar to Talbot's, but on hearing about daguerreotypes, he turned his attention to making direct positives in the camera. He succeeded too, but didn't make his methods known until 1840.

Briefly, his process was this: Making silver chloride paper similar to Talbot's, he then blackened it by the action of light before soaking it in potassium iodide and exposing it in a camera obscura. The process worked because when light struck the paper after its final coating, iodine separated from the potassium iodide and bleached the blackened paper, thus giving white highlights and leaving the already black paper for the shadows.

Yet despite the fact that so many were producing paper prints — some even before Talbot had produced his — the credit still rests firmly with him. Perhaps it is because Talbot was one of the few to recognise the necessity for having an intermediary negative. While others shunned negatives because they *were* negatives and not positives, Talbot saw the importance of being able to recreate the same picture over and over again from one master negative and it was this that no doubt led him to produce the first photographically illustrated book.

Pencil of Nature, written and illustrated by Talbot was published over the course of two years beginning in 1844. It comprised six volumes and the complete set contained twenty-four original calotypes, each one pasted in by hand. About 150 copies of each volume were produced and the prints were made at a special studio set up in Reading where paper negative originals were used to mass produce the illustrations.

The fixing of the finished calotypes, however, did not seem to have been carried out too well and many of the prints faded soon after the books were bought. It was criticism resulting from this fault that probably led Talbot to turn his talented mind to producing a more reliable method of mechanical photographic printing and by 1851, he had developed a photographic engraving process which was basically similar to that still used today and known as photogravure.

But that's another story.

4
Have darkroom, will travel

Of all the weird and wonderful concoctions dreamt up by inventors to help photography along its way, one of the strangest must have been a discovery made by Niépce's cousin, Abel Niépce de Saint-Victor. His rather curious finding was a photographic emulsion that used as its base the freshly-beaten white of a new-laid egg.

The result was the albumen process with which Saint-Victor took what is often credited as the first photograph on glass. Not so. True, his was the process which popularized glass plate photography, but it was a long way from being the first. Niépce used the bitumen process to take pictures on glass in 1829, as did Daguerre a few years later. And a decade before Saint-Victor's discovery, Sir John Herschel used a coating of silver bromide (sometimes iodide of chloride) on a glass plate, then washed it over with silver nitrate immediately before exposing it in the camera still wet. The resultant negative plate could be used either for printing positives onto paper or backed with a black background to give the appearance of a positive (the exposed emulsion reflected the light to show highlights, while the dark background showed through the clear glass to represent shadows.) Herschel used this latter method in 1839 to produce a picture which today is reckoned to be the earliest surviving photograph on glass.

In theory, Herschel's glass plates should have given far better positives than Talbot's paper negatives and yet it was the calotype that grew in popularity and glass plates took a back seat until 1847 when Saint-Victor arrived on the scene with his albumen process. This is how it worked:—

The white of a fresh egg was beaten until stiff when potassium iodide was added. The thick substance was then spread onto a glass plate and sensitized in a solution of silver nitrate and acetic acid. After exposure, the plate was developed in gallic acid, fixed, dried and printed in the same way as a calotype.

Photographers in general, however, weren't too enthusiastic. The process was very good for recording fine detail and the finished prints were better than the average calotype; the drawback was in the fact that exposures amounted

The Sutton Panoramic Camera. It was made by Ross and used Thomas Sutton's Panoramic Water Lens, patented in 1859. The lens was, in effect, a glass sphere filled with liquid and fitted with a central stop of f/12. It covered a field of view of 120 degrees and, to compensate for the curvature of field, the camera back had to be curved, resulting in a curved focusing screen, curved plates and — as the camera was built for the wet plate process — even a separate curved tank for sensitizing the plates.

The first picture on glass, taken by Sir John Herschel in 1839.

to anything up to fifteen minutes. The system was too slow and depended, believe it or not, on the freshness of the eggs. Even so, the albumen process did remain popular for some years in another form. The slowness that ruined its chances of success on plates didn't matter nearly so much when it was adapted for use on printing paper, and albumen paper remained popular as a substitute for silver chloride paper until the end of the century.

Thomas Box Tent mobile darkroom for the wet plate process.

Meanwhile, in another part of France, a French chemist was experimenting in a completely different field. Louis Ménard discovered that when guncotton was dissolved in a solution of ether and alcohol, it produced a viscous liquid that dried into a hard, transparent film. Ménard gave the substance a name. He called it collodion, but having discovered it, he could find no practical use for it. Doctors of the time, however, were ahead of him and used its hardening properties for dressing wounds.

It fell to Frederick Scott Archer, the son of an English butcher, to see the value of collodion for photographic purposes. Archer was a coin expert turned sculptor who learned the calotype process so that he could take photo-

Archer's Wet Plate camera designed in 1853. Sensitising and development could be carried out within the camera itself.

graphs of customers who wanted their busts modelled. Soon, the photography side of his work began to interest him more than modelling and it wasn't long before he started experimenting with the process.

His experiments led him to the use of collodion, but whereas others had used the substance because of its properties when dry, Archer took the unusual step of using it wet — and in so doing, he created a minor revolution in the history of photography and the camera. Archer perfected the process in 1850 and published its details a year later. Wet plate photography was destined to remain popular for another twenty years.

Suddenly, exposure times were cut to as little as five seconds, but photographers had to pay for this luxury with the effort needed to actually use the process. The plates had to be used wet and therefore needed to be made within minutes of their exposure in the camera. And for that, the photographer had to take a portable darkroom everywhere.

Archer himself designed a camera which was also a darkroom. By means of elasticated sleeves on its side, the photographer could carry out the complicated sensitizing and developing process actually inside the camera as well as making the exposure. But more usually, darkrooms were separate from the camera — sometimes carried on the photographer's back, occasionally mounted on a horse-drawn cart, but more often than not, loaded onto a sort of gigantic wheelbarrow. Here's how the wet plate process worked:-

First the photographer had to make his collodion. This he did by dropping cottonwool into a mixture of nitric acid and sulphuric acid which, after drying, gave him guncotton. He dissolved this in ether and alcohol to make collodion. Armed with this and much more besides, he loaded up his mobile darkroom and ventured forth.

Finding his subject, our photographer retired to his darkroom where he took a piece of glass and washed it thoroughly in alcohol and powdered pumice. A mixture of collodion and potassium iodide was then poured over the glass, tilting it carefully until the whole surface was evenly covered. Then, by the light of a candle, the plate was lowered into a bath of silver nitrate and water. Five minutes later, the plate was removed and examined. Only when it was a creamy white all over was it ready for the camera.

It was then exposed, still wet, and then taken back to the darkroom for development with pyrogallic acid before the collodion dried. It was fixed and washed in the normal way

35

Inside and out: the Dubroni
wet plate camera.

and the final print made on silver chloride or albumen
paper.

And if all that trouble for just one picture seems impos-
sibly complicated, remember that the Crimean War and the
American Civil War were both photographed by this process; and David Livingstone went on his famous travels with
a complete wet plate outfit.

The new method of photography on glass, despite its
clumsiness, soon caught on. Daguerreotypes and calotypes
that had previously been competing with one another
suddenly found themselves together in competition against
the new wet plate process and it soon became obvious which
of the three was going to win the day.

The cameras were ready and waiting. Any model that had
been used for daguerreotypes or calotypes was perfectly
suitable provided it was used with a wet plate dark slide, and
all that needed was four silver wires across the corners to
keep the plate in place and a gulley at the base to catch the
inevitable drips.

The cameras that grew up around the wet plate era are
difficult to put into any convenient category. They ranged
from a miniature built by T. Morris in 1859 which measured
a mere 4 x 4 x 5 cm and took portraits for lockets no more
than 2 cm square, to a camera built in 1860 by a Scottish
amateur named John Kibble. This one was enormous. The

plates measured 110 x 90 cm and the entire apparatus was mounted on a horse-drawn cart. Perhaps the size of the plates had something to do with Kibble's profession: he was a builder of greenhouses.

But despite the size of Kibble's camera, more and more people were turning their minds to making models more compact and portable. With so much to carry around in the way of chemicals and darkroom, the last thing they wanted was a bulky camera. Now the thing about all cameras is the fact that no matter how sophisticated they may be, they still represent what is essentially an empty box. So what could be more logical than to build a camera which, when not in use, could be folded flat.

In 1853, Thomas Ottewill of London made a 25 x 20 cm plate camera for landscape work in which the lens panel and focusing screen could be removed and the sides folded inwards in a V shape, to make a flat package 52.5 x 32.5 x 7.5 cm. In its working position, the camera was a sliding box design with a lens panel that slid vertically or horizontally — an early form of rising and crossing front.

Probably the biggest single revolution of the 1850s as far as camera design was concerned, was the introduction of the bellows. Not that there was anything really new about putting a folding leather bag between the lens panel and the plate; Niépce owned a crude version of just such a camera and there was a daguerreotype bellows camera back in 1839. But the wet plate era saw the bellows camera become a serious commercial proposition

A good example is the 1851 model made by the father and son team of William, William H. and Henry J. Lewis who were responsible for the first commercially produced bellows camera in America. It was, in fact, designed for the daguerreotype process and was consequently known as the Lewis Daguerreotype Camera, but it could of course equally be used for the wet plate process.

The Lewis camera measured 16 x 18 x 41 cm and had an f/4 lens of 15 cm focal length. It was made in two parts, a fixed lens panel linked by square bellows to the rear section, which took the form of a box capable of sliding backwards and forwards in a grooved base. The bellows were leather-covered fabric and the rest of the camera was made of veneered wood.

One of the first British bellows cameras was designed by the architect Captain Fowke and made by Ottewill. Front and back were joined by bellows, together with a brass rod to hold everything square. But for some reason best known to himself, Fowke designed a pyramid-shaped wooden box to hold the lens that stood out from the front of the bellows like a sore thumb. The result was both unnecessary and ungainly.

It was the time when cameras began to take on the traditional mahogany, leather and brass look which so typifies an old camera in the minds of most people; but there

38

were still one or two models that were totally unique in their design and the Pistolgraph was a perfect example. First developed by Thomas Skaife in 1856, the Pistolgraph was made of brass and took miniature plates 3.75 cm square. The camera took the form of a brass tube made in three telescopic sections for focusing and moulded to a square plate holder. Unlike many of the cameras of that time, the Pistolgraph had a shutter worked by rubber bands which gave an exposure of about 1/10 sec. What gave the camera its unusual appearance though was the fact that the whole thing was mounted on a ball and socket head which, in turn, was fixed to a small wooden box that could be used for storage of plates etc.

But surely one of the most sophisticated cameras of the time was the Dubroni whose name was an anagram of the man who invented it, a Frenchman named Bourdin. It comprised a camera and darkroom all in one; by no means the first, but definitely the neatest and most practical. The Dubroni first appeared in 1864. To look at, it was a wooden box measuring 7 x 8.75 x 8.75 cm with a lens on the front, a plate holder at the back and a rubber bulb on top. Inside, there was an earthenware container.

A collodion-coated plate was placed in the back and then the sensitizing solution introduced into the camera and onto the plate by means of a tube from the bulb. The camera was then tilted until the plate was evenly covered.

After exposure, developing, washing and fixing were also carried out inside the camera, using the tube and rubber bulb to insert and extract the solutions. The photographer could inspect the progress of his developing by holding the lens up to his eye and illumination for this came from a red window in the rear of the camera which, of course, had to be covered at the time of exposure.

Stereo cameras steadily grew in popularity during the wet plate era with models like J.B. Dancer's Stereocamera of 1856. This was a British sliding box camera designed for wet collodion plates but with a number of original features that equally allowed it to be used with collodio-albumen dry plates (dealt with in the next chapter). It became one of the earliest magazine cameras in which plates could be carried actually within the design. These were housed in wooden frames that rested in a box attached to the camera's base. They were lifted into the film plane by a metal rod that screwed into the top of the frame.

Each lens of the camera was covered by a circular disc with aperture stops graded one to five. A metal bar, pivoted at a point between the lenses, blocked the light from each and swung aside with a see-saw movement to form a crude type of shutter.

But stereo cameras of the time didn't necessarily have two lenses. The Moore Single Lens Stereocamera of 1865 for instance was basically a wooden box camera with a repeating back for taking two shots on a single plate. The whole assembly was mounted on a track fixed to the top of the camera's case. Between the two exposures, the camera was slid from one end of the track to the other and the repeating plate back slid into its alternative position. The result was a stereo pair on the same plate.

There were even stereo set-ups that consisted quite simply of two identical plate cameras mounted side by side and set at the right angle to produce a stereo pair, one picture from each camera. Most stereo cameras of the time, however, used two lenses.

Stereo cameras aside, the wet collodion process lent itself basically to a number of different end products, apart from straightforward prints. The ambrotype was one such. Although looked down upon by professional photographers who considered it to be nothing more than a cheap and cheerful imitation of the daguerreotype, the process became very popular for a while from about 1852 onwards.

An ambrotype was quite simply a wet plate negative that had been fixed with cyanide rather than hypo, treated with nitric acid or mercury bromide and then mounted against a dark background. The original dark tones of the negative were bleached by the treatment to an equivalent tone of white and the black background showed through the clear parts of the negative. The resulting picture was therefore seen as a positive.

A one-step collodion positive that didn't rely on the bleaching stage could also be made by developing the plate in iron sulphate, a chemical that gave a white image rather than the usual black. Mounted against a dark background, the end result was another form of ambrotype.

But like the daguerreotype, the ambrotype was another one-off process that used the plate from the camera for the finished picture and it gradually declined in popularity as a new craze swept through the photographic scene in the 1860s.

The thing that more than anything else killed the ambrotype was the carte-de-visite, portraits 5.6 x 8.75 cm mounted on a card 10 x 6.25 cm and used by friends as a personal kind of visiting card; hence, *carte-de-visite*. These

A set of four cartes-de-visite, one end product of the wet plate process.

were often taken on multiple lens cameras that took as many pictures on one plate as the camera had lenses, and sometimes the addition of a repeating back doubled the amount of pictures that could be taken at a single sitting.

It was an idea that caught on initially during the daguerreotype period when it was impossible to duplicate pictures and so getting a number of portraits on one plate was a distinct advantage. But even with wet plates, the actual process of producing prints from negatives was considered time-consuming and the fact that a number of identical portraits could be produced by contact printing one plate was considered a boon.

So the 1860s saw the popularization of cameras that sported two, four, even eight lenses. There was one, called the Dragon Microphotographic Camera that took 450 exposures 2 x 2 mm square on 4.5 x 8.5 cm wet plates by means of twenty-five lenses in combination with horizontal and vertical shifts of the front and back of the camera. This unique piece of equipment was, however, used for re-photographing negative plates to give a series of minute positives for mounting together with a viewing lens in a piece of jewellery or individual tiny viewer. Today, these minute pieces of photographica are known as Stanhopes after the Stanhope lens to which the microscopic pictures were fixed for viewing.

Multiple lens cameras were equally popular with ferrotype photographers for a process which was yet another variation on the wet collodion system. The ferrotype's nearest relation was the ambrotype and it was, in fact, introduced shortly after its glass cousin. It never did really achieve the popularity that the ambrotype enjoyed at its peak but, unlike the ambrotype, it held on for many years to come and ferrotype photography was still being practised long after the ambrotype was dead and gone.

The ferrotype was a form of positive collodion plate, but instead of being made on glass and mounted on a dark background, it was made directly onto black-enamelled tin. The process was cheap and nasty, the image vastly inferior to both the ambrotype and the daguerreotype that it vaguely resembled, but its virtues were that it was both quick and cheap, and it was soon taken up by seaside and carnival photographers who very often used cameras that were combined with processing units to give an on-the-spot portrait to customers in a matter of minutes.

Cameras for the ferrotype process ranged from the multiple lens models like the Lancaster Postage Stamp Camera of 1896 that took six 19mm square pictures, to others such as the single lens model made by Jonathan Fallowfield in 1890. This one took ferrotype pictures 4.5 x 6 cm which could be developed immediately after exposure in a tray at the base of the camera. It had an f/3.7 lens and a roller blind shutter.

The Aptus Ferrotype Camera made by the Liverpool firm of Moore and Co. in 1895 had a magazine on the base that held up to 100 sheets of sensitized tin plate. These were taken one at a time by a lever equipped with a suction device and held in the film plane for exposure, then dropped straight into a tray of developer.

The Aptus perfectly illustrates the strange appeal of the ferrotype process which never became truly popular and yet just refused to die. Because, strange as it may seem, there were models of the Aptus, not too different from the 1895 ancestors, still being built and sold by Moore and Co. as late as 1955.

The Ambrotype was another offshoot of the wet plate process . . .

. . . and the ferrotype or tintype was a third.

42

5

Photographic bowler hats

We now enter a period in the history of the camera that in many ways reads like an extract from a cookery book. We've already seen how new-laid eggs played their part in photography, now consider the following edible ingredients that found their way into the darkroom: beer, caramel, coffee, ginger wine, honey, liquorice, malt, milk, sherry, sugar, tea, treacle and vinegar. All these and more besides were used by researchers in an effort to get away from the cumbersome wet plate system and find something that would preserve sensitized plates in a dry or semi-dry state long enough for the photographer to be able to take pictures away from his darkroom.

The first practical dry collodion process came from a French chemist named Dr. J.M. Taupenot in 1855. His was the collodio-albumen process which relied on coating a collodion plate with iodized albumen and then dipping it in silver nitrate, thus giving two sensitized layers. In this state, the plate could be dried and kept for several weeks before use. The convenience, however, was somewhat negated by the loss of sensitivity; the dry plates were up to six times slower than their wet equivalent.

During the course of the following decade, numerous photographic processes came and went. Hardly a month passed without someone coming up with a new idea that just as quickly died.

But one thing was for certain: despite their lack of speed, dry plates were beginning to catch on and it wasn't long before a company was set up for the purpose of making and selling them to the public. For the first time, the photographer had no need to be a chemist. He could take a photograph without having to make his own plate beforehand. Instead, he could buy them dry over the counter and use them as and when needed for up to six months.

George Eastman is the man often credited with starting the first commercial dry plate company, but twenty-two years before Eastman began his business in 1880, an Englishman, Dr. Richard Hill set up the Patent Dry Collodion Plate Company in Birmingham and, by the end of 1858, he had forty agents throughout England and Canada who stocked and sold his plates.

And a camera for the process? How about the slightly unusual Photo-Binocular. Made in the style of a pair of binoculars with one lens as camera and the other as viewfinder, the camera held a drum-shaped magazine with fifty dry collodion plates inside.

This magazine could be clipped to the camera immediately prior to exposure when a plate was dropped into the plane of focus. The magazine was then removed, the exposure made and the magazine clipped on again to drop the plate back into its receptacle. A knob on the side of the drum brought the next plate into position for loading again.

The only drawback was the lengthy exposure time. Since the camera looked like a pair of binoculars, you would be forgiven for assuming it could be hand held. But you'd be wrong. The Photo-Binocular had to be used on a tripod which rather defeated its own object.

A major advance came in 1864 with the first commercial emulsion; silver bromide already mixed with collodion so that photographers could make their own dry plates by simply pouring the mixture over a sheet of glass and using it

The 'MB' No. 4, made by Harlow Brothers of Birmingham.

dry. For the first time, no silver bath was needed for sensitizing.

And yet, even with all the progress that was being made, photographers were still basically on the wrong track. Although the plates being made both professionally and by amateurs were now dry, they were still no more than dry equivalents of wet plates; they still relied for their success on collodion. And they were still very slow.

Then came the innovation which, in many ways, was the last, because it marked the start of a system we still use today. The man responsible was Richard Leach Maddox; his invention was the gelatine dry plate.

Gelatine, a jelly-like substance made from the bones and hides of cattle, had actually been used by Hill in his commercially produced plates, but only in association with collodion.

Other people, including Saint-Victor, had experimented with the substance, but to Maddox goes the credit for making the process work. Whereas so many before him had used gelatine as an aid to preserving collodion, Maddox took the brave step of using it *instead* of collodion.

His emulsion consisted of gelatine containing nitric and hydrochloric acids, cadmium bromide and the ever present

Two early dry plate cameras: A Lancaster International of 1887 (right) and an unmarked tailboard camera from the same era.

silver nitrate. It was coated onto glass, used dry and developed in pyrogallic acid and silver nitrate.

With this almost deceptively simple method of plate making, Maddox changed the history of picture-taking, and yet the strange thing was that he seemed to lose interest in the idea as soon as it was made public, leaving any improvement that could be made to others. Two years later, in 1873, John Burgess, an English photographer, adapted Maddox's methods to his own ends and offered the first commercial gelatine process for sale. Photographers bought his product, made their own plates with it and, for the first time, found they had a dry plate with the speed of a wet plate.

From there, it was only a short step to turn the production of gelatine dry plates into a commercial enterprise. By 1878, four English manufacturers were offering the new plates for sale and it wasn't long before the news spread across the Atlantic. In America, a 24-year-old bank clerk began experimenting with photographic emulsions, using information he had gathered from England. By 1879, he had invented his own emulsion coating machine and in 1880, he began mass producing plates in a small rented loft at Rochester in New York.

Studio camera made by Meagher circa 1890.

The man's name was George Eastman and the business he started was destined to become one of the great names in photography today. The company which Eastman started with Henry Strong was known as the Eastman Dry Plate Company. But although the famous name wouldn't be dreamt up for some years to come, that business, started there in a rented loft, was the beginning of Kodak. Of which, more later.

Let's turn our attention to the cameras of the day.

With the new freedom offered by dry plates, camera styles quickly took off in a number of different directions, but they fall mainly into two categories: field cameras, mostly large, a little cumbersome and rarely used without a tripod; and hand cameras which, as the name implies, could be hand-held.

An example of the mousetrap type of shutter.

Let's look first at an early field camera that became a classic design on which many manufacturers were to base their ideas. It came from the mind of George Hare, an early associate of Ottewill.

In 1882, Hare designed a bellows camera with the back hinged to the baseboard and the lens board fitted to a movable panel within that baseboard, allowing the lens to be set anywhere along its path. Rack and pinion control gave precise focusing and the camera could be folded after use by sliding the lens panel into the back and then folding the baseboard up to meet it.

A variation on Hare's theme produced the tailboard camera. In this, the front panel was hinged in a fixed position to the baseboard and the back fixed to any one of a number of positions in a panel that again slid within that baseboard. For folding, the back was brought up flush against the rear of the lens panel and the base, hinged at the appropriate point, folded to meet it, thus protecting the ground-glass screen.

The third variation on the folding design employed movement of both front and back of the camera and was folded after use by dropping the front into the camera's base and then bringing the whole assembly up to meet the back.

If the lens board could be extended on its movable panel beyond the length of the baseboard, the camera was said to have a double extension; movement of the back beyond the baseboard as well gave the camera triple extension.

A perfect example of a typical field camera was the Lancaster Instantograph of 1886. Like George Hare's design of four years previous, the back was hinged to the base which folded down to allow the lens panel to travel along its length. By 1888, the Instantograph was offered in four sizes from 8 x 10.5 cm up to 25 x 30 cm.

The Instantograph was a square bellows camera. Like all

A Lancaster Instantograph of 1886.

47

early models, the bellows were four-sided and folded with 90 degree corners which put considerable strain on the leather, often resulting in tiny holes. But in the years that followed, a new method of folding became popular. Corners were nipped in to make bellows that were actually eight-sided, four of which were extremely short and providing corners with two 45 degree folds, rather than one of 90 degrees.

Before leaving field cameras and venturing into the various types of hand camera, it might be advisable to pause at this point and consider one of the accessories that was becoming more and more popular around this time. While it is not the intention of this book to look at camera accessories in too much detail, this particular piece of equipment can hardly be ignored. Because what started off as an accessory quickly became a necessity. We're talking about the shutter.

As plates increased in speed, it became obvious that a more accurate method of making exposures was going to be needed. No longer was it possible to time an exposure by removing the lens cap, counting three and replacing it. Something far more precise was needed.

The first shutters were completely independent of the camera. They were bought separately and simply fixed to the front of the lens. In an early design, a box contained a blind that ran over a roller. As the photographer pulled a string attached to the end of the blind, it lifted to allow light through the lens, while the opposite end of the blind travelled down the other side and closed the gap again. The faster the string was pulled, the briefer the exposure.

Another design opened and closed a flap for whatever time was required, the timing again judged by the photographer. From there, it was a simple step to make the flap open by a pneumatic cylinder operated by squeezing a rubber bulb. (It's rather quaint to realize that even now the 'open shutter' setting on modern cameras is still represented by the letter B which originally stood for this bulb.)

Soon shutters began to get more mechanical. A see-saw arrangement of two holes passing the lens was one type and a rotating disc was another. More often than not, these were powered by rubber bands.

Not that all shutters were successful. Some even defeated their own object, operating so violently that they induced camera shake during the actual exposure.

By far the most popular type of shutter found around the time of early dry plate cameras was one that came to be known as the mousetrap; a roller blind type made, among others, by Thornton Pickard. The principle was as simple as it was effective. A flat wooden box held a fabric blind with a gap in it suspended between two rollers. The rollers were sprung and could be tensioned to give an exposure which was usually anything between 1/15 and 1/90 sec.

The shutter was set by pulling a chord which tensioned the spring. It was released by a lever which could be worked by hand or rubber bulb. Mousetrap shutters came in two different types; one that fitted snugly over the front of the lens and another that fixed to the camera and allowed the lens to be screwed into its front.

The focal plane shutter arrived in the mid-1890s and, like the others, it was first designed as a separate accessory, but one that the manufacturer tailored to fit individual cameras on a slightly more permanent basis. The shutter took the form of a roller blind with a wide slit in it. The photographer had two adjustments to play with; one controlled the speed with which the slit travelled across the plate, the other varied the width of the slit itself. The blind also had provision for a plate-sized gap that was brought into play for focusing.

Then came mechanical and metal between-the-lens shutters such as those produced by Bausch and Lomb in 1891. Exposure on these was governed by metal blades that opened and closed, usually at settings from around 1 to 1/100 sec. In some cases, one set of blades controlled both shutter speed and aperture.

It was these mechanical between-the-lens shutters that were usually found on hand cameras. Which leads us very neatly back to our second category of early dry plate camera.

The basic idea of a hand camera was to take the instrument away from the tripod and make it possible to use it in the hand, and that meant finding a way of using the camera without a focusing screen. So the camera would need first a viewfinder, and second a focusing scale of some sort. Many makers seemed to believe that the addition of these two refinements on a model that was smaller than the average field camera automatically turned it into a hand camera. They were, to say the least, optimistic.

Plates were getting faster all the time, but in many cases they still weren't fast enough for hand-held exposures, and a tripod, while not a necessity, was still a distinct advantage. Which is why we more often hear these early examples referred to as *hand and stand* cameras. They could be used either way, but there's no prizes for guessing which produced the better results.

So the first hand cameras were nothing more than smaller versions of their field camera cousins, with the addition of a viewfinder and a focusing scale.

But as plates grew faster and more reliable, cameras did become truly portable and that was when numerous styles of hand cameras began to appear. There were magazine cameras that held perhaps a dozen plates all loaded and ready for use inside the camera, and in these, plates were changed after each exposure by all sorts of clever and ingenious methods.

Above right: the Ben Akiba Photographic Cane.

Fallowfield's Facile Camera of 1887 is a good example. In this, plates were loaded into a box on top of the camera and, after exposure, were moved to a corresponding box in the base.

Magazine cameras, as we shall see later, were extensively developed and improved upon during the 1890s in an attempt to challenge the growing interest in roll film.

But perhaps more than anything else, this was the time of the miniature, a time when cameras not only became smaller, but took on many weird and wonderful shapes that a few years previously would never have been associated with cameras at all. It was a time when detectives were coming into vogue. In fiction, Sherlock Holmes was beginning to show his face, in America, the famous Pinkerton Agency was making news. *Detective* was the in word and it wasn't long before it became applied to cameras.

In general, detective cameras were either models small and convenient enough to be hidden at the moment a picture was being taken or cameras that were quite blatantly styled to look like something else. This last type, while known by the overall title of detective cameras, should more properly be termed *concealed cameras*.

A good example of a straightforward detective camera that was not necessarily a concealed camera, was Schmid's Patent Detective Camera which, in 1884, introduced Americans to the style. It was in the shape of a small box 11 x 15.5 x 22 cm. External shutter controls and a focusing scale that could be used without so much as glancing at a ground-glass screen gave photographers the freedom to take a picture without using something that spelt CAMERA in large letters to onlookers who could then be easily photographed without their knowledge.

Right: the Ticka watch-type camera with optional extra viewfinder attached.

In England, there was a model made by the London firm of Watson and Sons in 1886. This was basically a quarter-plate bellows camera fitted into a leather-covered box equipped with two viewfinders — one on the top and another on the side. Inside the box and at the back of the camera there was a space large enough to hold some dark slides loaded with plates.

Earlier still was the cheap and cheerful Demon made in America in 1878. It held only a single dry plate and once the picture had been taken, it needed a darkroom or changing bag before the next could be considered; a fact that the manufacturers seemed to gloss over in their advertisements of the time:-

Defies detection and can be secreted under vest, in the watch pocket or concealed in the glove. No movement is too rapid for it — the race-horse at greatest speed, the flight of birds, even the lightning flash itself. No knowledge of photography necessary. It requires no focusing, no stand, no adjustment, no dark slides; yet hundreds of plates can be carried and exposed in rapid succession.

Most small or unobtrusive cameras of the time were referred to as detective cameras, but surely the most interesting models were the concealed cameras. As each manufacturer tried to outdo his rival, cameras arrived on the market disguised as bowler hats, shoes, watches, books, walking sticks, tie-pins, shirt buttons, neck-ties, revolvers, binoculars, handbags, drinking cups, Gladstone bags, purses and even things like German sausages and Swiss rolls.

Possibly the best known was the Stirn, made in 1886 and invented by New Yorker Robert D. Gray. The camera was

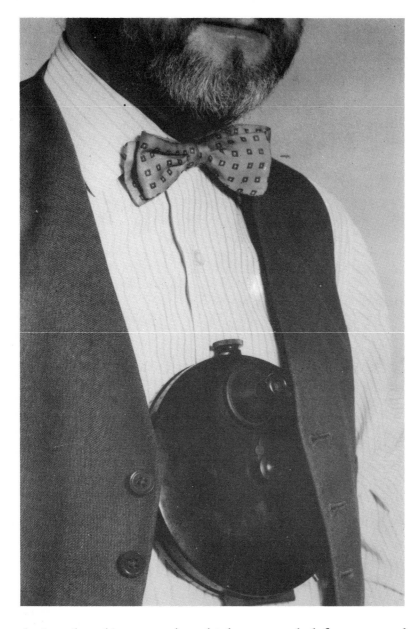

designed to be worn chest-high, suspended from a cord around the photographer's neck. He would wear it under his shirt or waistcoat with the lens poking out through a button-hole. Exposures were made by pulling a small ring at the bottom of the device and then, as a central knob was turned, the next plate was brought into position and the shutter tensioned all in one movement. It took six exposures on special circular plates.

The Necktie Camera or Photo-Cravate came from France in 1840. This was a long, oblong device hidden in a cravat that the suspicious person might have noticed having a lens sticking through where a pin might normally have been found. A small, round knob protruding from the bottom was attached to a cycle chain which brought one of six plates into position for each exposure. The exposure itself was carried out by means of a pneumatic bulb secreted in the trousers pocket.

The Hat Camera was the speciality of the Adams Company among others and was fitted into the top of any standard bowler. It was used by removing the hat and aiming the camera, holding the brim close against the chest.

Then there was the Kreugner Patent Book Camera of 1887. This was actually bound in morocco to look like a

Above: the Kreugner Book Camera.

Right: the Magic Photoret.

53

typical novel of the day. The lens that looked out through the spine was an f/16 meniscus type and the camera had a single speed shutter operated by a string.

Surely the most frightening of the concealed cameras must have been Thomson's Revolver Camera made in 1862. It held tiny plates in the bullet chamber, had a lens down the barrel and exposure was made — as if you hadn't guessed — by pulling the trigger.

But one of the most popular styles of concealed camera was that disguised as a watch. The Lancaster Company introduced theirs in 1887. When closed, the camera looked like a pocket watch of the day; but pressing a spring on the side shot a series of telescopic tubes into position, much like opening a tiny bellows camera.

According to Lancaster's advert: *The lens is a very rapid one and can be adjusted for taking portraits, groups or views etc.*

The watch camera was one of the few designs of concealed camera that made the transition from plates to film, and although we are not dealing with film as such in this chapter, no history of the concealed camera would be complete without mention of one of the most popular. The appropriately named Ticka was made by Houghton in 1907 and it was a watch camera with the lens concealed in the 'winding mechanism'. Yet the really revolutionary thing about the Ticka was not its shape, but its film; 16mm wide, backed with paper and fed from one cardboard cassette to another. It could almost have been the blueprint for today's 110 cameras.

Other watch-type cameras included the Magic Photoret of 1893, The Expo Watch Camera of 1904 and even as late as 1949, a wristwatch version called the Steineck ABC.

The latter part of the 19th Century was, without a doubt, a time for camera innovation. Field cameras, hand cameras, miniature cameras, detective cameras . . . there was something to suit everyone and every purpose. It seems impossible that any other major design could possibly have been squeezed into so short a space of time. And yet, before the Century was out, three more important styles of camera, two of which are still with us today, had arrived.

In 1861, the first single lens reflex was patented, 1882 saw the arrival of the first twin lens reflex and in 1897, the first colour camera was built.

In the 1861 design by Thomas Sutton, a mirror reflected the lens's image onto a screen in the top of the camera. To expose a plate in the back of the camera, the mirror was flipped out of the light path by turning a knob on the side and this action also acted as a crude form of shutter. But although Sutton designed and patented his idea in 1861, evidence points to the fact that the camera was never built. Probably the earliest single lens reflex to actually appear on the market was one made by E. W. Smith of New York and patented in 1884. Other single lens reflexes of the time included names like the Vanneck, Gambier and Miral — all from the 1890s.

Marion's Academy camera of 1882 is usually recognised as the first twin lens reflex. The camera featured two lenses — one for taking, the other for viewing — mounted one above the other. The viewing lens projected its image onto a ground-glass screen at the back of the camera immediately above the plate. On the base of the camera, a small magazine held twelve plates that could be moved along by means of a rack and pinion. When the first plate was in position directly below the plane of focus, the camera was inverted so that the plate fell into its rightful place. Then it was dropped back into the magazine after exposure and the magazine moved up another notch for the next plate.

The camera was finished in polished wood with an f/5, 50mm lens and rotary shutter. Like so many of its contemporaries, it summed up the precision and sheer inventiveness of the age.

Cameras designed for taking colour pictures date from 1874 when Louis Ducos du Hauron patented the Chromographoscope, built eventually in 1897. But although this can be considered as probably the first colour camera, it was by no means responsible for producing the first colour photograph.

Colour photography had been tried and even proved possible right back at the start when Niépce produced that first heliotype in 1826. There is evidence to show that he and Daguerre actually succeeded in taking colour photographs of a kind, though they never discovered a way to fix them and so no substantial proof of their claims exists today. Neither is it clear what methods they used.

In 1839, Herschel actually obtained a coloured photograph of the spectrum with which he forecast the possibility of serious colour photography; but again there was no way of fixing his image.

The man who eventually set colour photography on the right track was an Englishman named James Clerk Maxwell. In 1861, at London's Royal Institute, he showed for the first time how the human eye was sensitive to only three colours — red, blue and green — and that all other colours were no more than combinations of these three primaries.

Maxwell had three black and white lantern slides made of the same subject, a tartan ribbon. Each plate was taken through a filter of one of the primary colours. The plates were projected, each with their appropriate filter in front of the lens. The three images were superimposed on a screen and the result was a colour picture.

The way was now clear for colour cameras to be made. What was needed was a single camera that could take three exposures on three different plates through three different filters — all at the same time. The Chromographascope was the first. In this, a system of straight mirrors and semi-reflecting mirrors allowed the lens's image to be reflected around the camera onto three different plates, each through one of the primary colours. The camera was also used as a viewer when the developed plates were put back in their appropriate places.

This was followed by similar cameras such as the Melano-chromoscope of 1899; and models such as that made by Lancaster for E. T. Butler in 1905 which used a Compound shutter, f/6.3 lens and bellows for focusing.

Colour cameras were many and various, but all relied on the one basic precept: they were all methods of producing three different images of the subject. It was another few years before the inventors realized that they were on the wrong track. What was really needed was not so much a special camera, as a special plate — one that could be used in any ordinary camera of the day to make a coloured image. And that wasn't as far off as might be expected.

Jos-Pe one-shot colour camera.

6

You press the button,
we do the rest

Towards the end of the 19th Century, one man did more to popularise photography and cameras for the man in the street than anyone else before him. His name was George Eastman.

We've already seen Eastman as one of the early pioneers in gelatine dry plate manufacture, but there was a great deal more to the man that that. In the years that followed the start of his dry plate business, he turned his attention to the possibilities of roll film and in 1885, he introduced the Eastman-Walker roller slide, a device that clipped onto the back of a conventional plate camera in place of the plate holder and held a twenty-four exposure roll of paper film. After exposure, the emulsion-coated paper was developed and then oiled to make it transparent for printing.

A year later, in 1886, Eastman began making his roller slides for use with a new type of paper-based film called stripping film and although he wasn't the first to use it, he *was* the first to use it extensively; first in his roller slide and later in a camera.

Eastman's own brand of stripping film consisted of a layer of soluble gelatine laid down on a paper base, followed by a layer of collodion and then a sensitized gelatine emulsion. After exposure, the film was developed and fixed in the usual way, then attached to a glass plate coated with glycerine. Hot water was then poured over the paper, the soluble gelatine melted and the paper stripped off, leaving the image behind on the glass. Finally, the now reversed image was transferred to a damp sheet of gelatine, from which the final print was made in the usual way.

The process was both messy and complicated, and yet it was with this that Eastman launched his first camera. His aim was a model which would bring photography within easy reach of everyone, a simple camera that anyone could use anywhere at any time — given, of course, the right lighting conditions.

The Kodak, together with a picture taken by this first roll film camera.

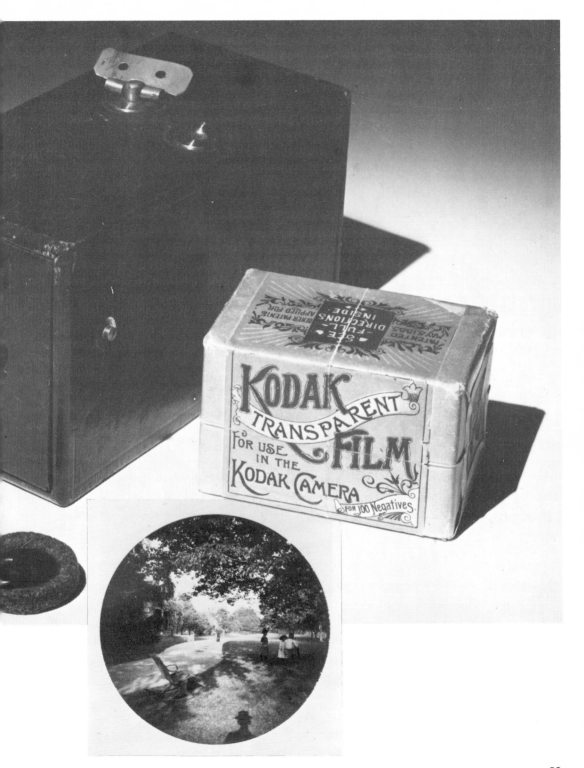

𝒯HE 𝒦ODAK

Is the smallest, lightest, and simplest of all Detective Cameras—for the ten operations necessary with most Cameras of this class to make one exposure, we have **only 3 simple** movements.

NO FOCUSSING.   NO FINDER REQUIRED.

Size 3¼ by 3¾ by 6½ inches.   **MAKES 100 EXPOSURES.**   Weight 35 ounces.

Setting the Shutter.   Exposing.   Winding more Film.   Cutting off Exposure.

Removing the Roller Slide.

Drawing off Exposed Films.

Cutting off Exposures.

Developing 12 at once.   Placing New Roll of 100 in position.

Placing Film in Roller Slide.

Examining Negatives (three on one strip).

Complete Kodak.

Carrying Case.

Full Information Furnished by

THE EASTMAN DRY PLATE & FILM Co., 115, Oxford St., London, W.

Eastman launched his camera with a previously unheard of name that was destined to live on well after the camera and long after Eastman himself. His idea was to find a truly distinctive trademark. He wanted a short, sharp word that could be easily pronounced, had no current meaning in any language and was difficult to miss-spell. He eventually came up with a completely new word that was as unusual as it was distinctive and with this, in 1888, he launched his camera.

He called it simply, *The Kodak.*

This original model was a box camera less than 18cm long that took 100 exposures at one loading. It had a fixed focus lens and a fixed shutter speed of around 1/25 sec — fast enough to allow hand-held exposures, slow enough to register on the slow film. It took circular negatives 6.25cm in diameter that utilized the whole of the lens's projected image.

But the thing that appealed to Mr. Average was the camera's extreme simplicity. Eastman launched his new era in photography with the slogan, *You press the button, we do the rest* and that really summed up the whole process. The camera sold for $25 (about £10 at that time) which included an already loaded film. Taking a picture was easy. A string cocked the shutter, a button released it and a key on the top wound on the film.

When the 100 exposures were finished, the photographer sent the whole camera back to the works where it was unloaded and the film developed and printed. The first roll of film was processed free and the enclosure of $10 (£4) guaranteed that a new roll of processed-paid film would be found loaded in the sealed camera on its return.

In the same year as The Kodak was launched, an English photographer, then living in America, introduced emulsion-coated celluloid in the form of cut film of various sizes. And eighteen months before that, the Rev. Hannibal Goodwin had applied for a patent on a similar idea applied to flexible roll film. The patent, however, was not granted at that time. It fell to Eastman to actually make the idea viable and in 1889, The Kodak was sold with a celluloid roll film in place of the less practical stripping film.

The fact that Eastman's company had actually won a patent a few years *after* Goodwin's application led to a law suit which, after twelve years in the courts, ended in Eastman having to pay out the sum of $5,000,000. As the price for a world monopoly on the most practical method ever of taking photographs, Eastman must have considered the sum worthwhile. Transparent flexible film began a new

The Kombi: camera and viewer combined.

Inside and out: the Mersey
falling plate camera.

Ontoscope stereo camera.

A full-plate Sanderson . . . and
an example of its versatility.

era in photography and one that has not been superseded
even today.

But although Eastman was always the great innovator, he
was by no means the only one in the field. It was a time for
eager competition between camera manufacturers and the
fact that Eastman held the rights to make celluloid roll film
did nothing to deter rival companies from coming up with
new camera designs of their own. In the same year as The
Kodak switched to celluloid film, the Boston Camera
Company introduced their Hawk-Eye Camera, a box design
that featured adjustable bellows within its body and which

gave the user the best of all possible worlds in its choice of sensitive material: single exposures could be made on 10 x 12.5cm dry plates or cut film and 100 exposures could be made at one loading on roll film.

Not that all new designs took roll film. There were still plenty of plate cameras about and new designs were appearing every day. Jumelle cameras were a popular style of the 1890s. They took their name from the fact that their distinctive style was that of a squat pyramid, rather like a pair of binoculars enclosed in a case — and the French for *binocular* is *jumelle*.

The first Photo-Jumelle appeared in 1890 and was built by a scientific instrument maker named Jule Carpentier. It took the form of a pair of binoculars with one lens for taking the picture and the other acting as viewfinder. The camera was commercially produced in 1892 and took twelve 4.5 x 6cm dry plates in a magazine.

Although the name *jumelle* was originally applied to twin lens cameras of this style, it eventually came to refer to any camera of a tapering design that looked vaguely like a pair of binoculars. Such a camera was the Photo-Etui-Jumelle of 1893, which took single exposures on 9 x 12cm plates or the Steno-Jumelle of 1894 that held eighteen plates in a magazine and had a direct vision viewfinder mounted on top of the body.

The late 1890s and early 1900s saw a tremendous rise in the popularity of stereo cameras as manufacturers everywhere began producing stereo counterparts of their standard models. The jumelle type of course made the most obvious choice for such adaptation, being already based on opera glasses and therefore the perfect design for a two lens camera.

The Bazin et Leroy Stereocycle of 1898 was a good example. It actually looked like a pair of rather square binoculars. Not so the Bellieni Jumelle being made about the same time. This was a box form camera with a magazine back to hold thirty-six 8 x 9cm plates. As well as a rising and crossing front, the camera sported six-speed rotary shutters on each of the f/8 lenses.

Meanwhile, George Eastman, never a man to rest on his laurels, was pressing on in new directions. after his first Kodak, he introduced the No. 2 (only then did his original camera become known as the No. 1). This second generation Kodak took the larger picture size of 8.75cm. Then, in 1890, he introduced the first Kodak Folding Cameras: the No. 3, No. 3 Junior, No. 4 and No. 4 Junior. These were in the style of a box with one side that dropped down to support a lens that slid out of the box on bellows.

The first Folding Pocket Kodak.

Like the first models, the film for these folding models was loaded and processed at the factory. But then, in 1891, Eastman's company marketed a daylight-loading camera, together with roll film that could be loaded or unloaded for the first time by the customer. The new cameras were larger and had larger lenses that for the first time on a Kodak camera necessitated the use of a focusing scale.

Of course, while Eastman held the rights on roll film, he enjoyed the best of both worlds. Every new roll film camera designed by a rival company merely meant more sales for his film. But although roll film presented possibly the most significant advance to date, it was by no means the cheapest and, compared with plates, the quality still left a lot to be desired.

The Frena camera introduced by R. and J. Beck in 1892 used neither roll film nor plates. It took celluloid cut film in packs of twenty or forty, arranged like a pack of cards with a piece of opaque card between each sheet. When the pack was loaded into the camera, a mechanism within matched up to alternate notches in the film sheets, allowing each to drop into a chamber on the back of the camera after exposure, while holding the rest ready for the following exposures.

But despite its drawbacks, roll film was catching on and being adapted to a number of different types of camera. The Kombi appeared in 1894. It was a tiny box camera only 4 x 4 x 5.5cm that took twenty-five exposures at a time on specially spooled roll film only 3cm wide. But the feature that made the Kombi so unusual was the fact that it could also be used as a viewer. A panel was removed from the camera's back and the pictures, wound through on the film rollers, could be viewed through the lens.

Another unusual adaptation of roll film came from France in the same year. The Cyclographe was a panoramic camera

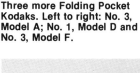

Three more Folding Pocket Kodaks. Left to right: No. 3, Model A; No. 1, Model D and No. 3, Model F.

Inside and out: the Kodak Panoram.

that revolved on a clockwork motor through anything up to 360 degrees, while the film moved in the opposite direction. The result was a negative 8.5 cm wide and up to 80 cm long.

The following year, in 1895, Eastman introduced another new model from his works. The pocket Kodak was a box camera, but one that featured an idea that to many seemed revolutionary. For the first time in a Kodak camera, the film was backed with paper which was numbered. The numbers could be read through a small red window in the camera's back as the film was wound from one exposure to the next. This new idea was known as cartridge film.

Such is Eastman's reputation for inventiveness that he is often credited with being the first to introduce the red window idea; but in fact he was using it under licence at that time from the Boston Camera Manufacturing Company

66

who introduced the idea three years earlier in a box camera of their own called the Bulls-Eye. In the end, the red window became such an essential part of camera design that Eastman bought out his rivals rather than pay them royalties on every camera he produced. He then carried on making the Bulls-Eye under the Kodak name.

Roll film was being used and adapted to many different ends and yet, strange as it may seem, 1895 also saw the birth of one of the most famous and versatile plate cameras ever produced. We're talking about the Sanderson.

Its designer, Frederick Sanderson, was a cabinet maker and stone mason. He was interested in both photography and architecture. It was when he tried to combine his two interests, using cameras of the day, that he ran into trouble. Converging verticals and distortion may actually enhance a pictorial worker's picture, and of course, neither is a problem to the portraitist. But if, like Sanderson, you wanted to make an accurate record of a building, then you needed something more than a straightforward field camera. A rising front, of course, helped and crude versions of these were around in Sanderson's day, but it by no means solved all his problems.

And so, like many others, Sanderson set out to design a camera for his own personal needs and found he had invented a classic that was to become a historic milestone in the history of the camera.

What Sanderson did was take a basic field camera design and modify it so that the lens panel was supported in four slotted arms — two on each side of the body pivoted on the extending panel within the base. The four arms were made to move independently and the lens designed to slide up and down them, to be locked in any position along that movement, including out of square to the plate if necessary. The result was a camera with a full range of rise and fall, swing and tilt; all controlled by two knobs on the side of the lens panel, while the photographer watched the result on the ground-glass screen.

Later models were fitted with a tallbody feature which meant the back of the camera was made slightly taller than usual to accommodate the bellows when the rising front was at the top of its throw.

The plate camera was a long way from being dead and many manufacturers still maintained that plates would win out in the end. Even so, roll film did give photographers a number of exposures on a single loading and that, it had to be admitted, was an advantage. So rather than build cameras to take Eastman's film, the plate manufacturers came up with a compromise. The result was the falling plate camera, a very simple magazine style that became immensely popular in the 1890s.

The camera was a box design. A number of plates were held in plate holders stacked in the back of the camera one behind the other and held tightly together by a large spring in the camera's back. Moving a knob on the top of the

A Kodak Cirkut, together with one of its panoramic pictures. The original print is 90cm wide.

camera operated a catch that allowed the front plate to fall into the camera's base while holding the next in position for the following exposure.

Shutters were simple and single-speeded as a rule, and focusing, when included in the design, was often by a series of supplementary lenses that slid into position in front of the taking lens. Falling plate cameras could be bought for as little as £3 in the 1890s and by 1900, manufacturers had their prices down to as little as £1.

Compared to Eastman's Kodaks, they were cheap, but Eastman knew when he was onto a winning streak and, ignoring the opposition, he pushed ahead with new designs of his own. In 1898, he introduced the Folding Pocket Kodak, the first camera with an all-metal case. It took 5.7 x 8.3cm negatives and the lens panel was supported on hinged arms that folded back into the body, making a flat box 16.25cm long by 3.75cm thick which was easily slipped into a pocket. The shutter had two separate controls for time and instantaneous exposures.

Two more models of the same basic design were introduced in 1899, the year that Kodak also came up with a panoramic camera. The Kodak Panoram took five photographs on a roll of film, each one 8.75 x 19.5cm. A touch of the shutter release caused the lens to swing through 142 degrees, exposing the film as it went.

The same year saw the introduction of an unusual American miniature called the Presto which could be used with 3cm plates or roll film. An elipse-shaped metal box in design, it had a gravity shutter that was set by simply turning the camera upside down.

But how ever much we stray to other makers, we must return time and time again during these years to George Eastman. In 1900, a No. 3 version of the Folding Pocket Kodak appeared and took quarter-plate roll film. It was this model that took on the shape with which folding cameras

Kodak Folding Brownie.

The all metal Presto.

Two Vest Pocket Kodak cameras. The one above is fitted with an autographic back.

A Zeiss Ikon strut camera.

Front and back: Three Autographic Kodak cameras.

The Ensignette.

would be associated for another half century or more. Pioneered by Kodak, copied by so many others, the design took the original flat box and added a hinged baseboard one-third the way along its front. When folded down, the lens panel was pulled out along it and, although the camera could easily be used in the horizontal position, it is in the vertical position, with the baseboard supported on its small metal leg that we most often think of the style.

So the new century began. Camera making became a highly mechanised business. Metal took the place of wood, and shutters, already recognised as necessities rather than luxuries, became more sophisticated with each new model that appeared.

With the start of the Century, came a new name that moved straight into the history books as 1900 saw the arrival

71

of the first Brownie, a box camera aimed at bringing photography to the up and coming generation of boys and girls who previously had only ever seen dad using a camera. The name was chosen deliberately to appeal to the youngsters and the cardboard box in which this basically simple box camera was sold decorated with pictures of imps.

The early part of the 20th Century was a time when the first amateur enlargers began appearing on the scene, but at the very beginning of the Century, the only real way to get a big image was to use a big plate, and in America in 1900, the idea was taken to almost ridiculous lengths.

The officials of the Chicago and Alton Railroad Company wanted a picture of their newest luxury train for the Paris Exposition. They wanted the picture to be impressive, perfect in every detail, but, most of all, they wanted it to be BIG. So they commissioned a special camera to be built for the purpose.

The Goerz Tenax with film pack holder and double dark slides.

What they got was a monster called the Mammoth, reputed to be the world's largest camera.

The Mammoth, 4 metres long and operated by a team of fifteen men, weighed 1,400 lbs. It was moved about the country on a specially made railway truck. Developing the 500 lb plate took 10 gallons of chemicals and the resultant image was 1.4 x 2.4 metres.

The judges at the Paris Exposition were so overwhelmed that they awarded the subsequent picture of the train *Grand Prize of the World*. After which, having done its job, the Mammoth was quietly dismantled and never seen again.

In 1903, the first practical method of colour photography was patented by Louis and Auguste Lumiere. It was called the Autochrome process. While we are dealing more with cameras than processes in this book, it might be as well to pause here to look at this particular method since it enabled photographers for the first time to take colour photographs with their everyday conventional cameras, rather than using the special separation models that had been needed up until then. The process was put on the market in 1907 and briefly, this is how it worked:-

Minute grains of potato starch were dyed, each one orange, green or violet. These were then sorted together so that each of the three colours was present in an equal proportion and then scattered over a glass plate, nearly 10,000 particles to the square millimetre. When pressed, they then formed a lamination of tiny coloured filters. The gaps between the grains were dusted with charcoal so that light could penetrate the plate only through the grains and the whole thing was then covered with a transparent varnish.

This was then coated with a panchromatic emulsion and the plate slotted into the camera, glass side towards the lens, so that the starch grains were acting as primary coloured filters in front of the emulsion. A yellow filter was placed over the lens and the exposure made.

The plate was developed in the normal way and then further developed to make a positive. With the starch grains still intact, the plate was then held up to the light or placed in a viewer, when a true representation of colours would be seen.

The Autochrome process was the most positive step that had yet been taken in colour photography and it proved tremendously popular. By 1913, the Lumiere factories were making up to 6,000 Autochrome plates a day and production actually continued until as late as 1932 when the firm adapted their process from plates to roll film. The result was Lumicolor.

Back to Kodak. In 1904, the first folding Brownie appeared, a horizontally styled folding camera, this time with a baseboard that dropped down from the centre of a flat oblong box. The folding Brownies, made after a year in two sizes, were distinguished by their red bellows and polished wood lens mounts.

In 1906, Kodak introduced a new panoramic camera called the Cirkut. Its principle was totally different to their earlier Panoram. Mounted on its own specially made tripod, the Cirkut was capable of revolving a full 360 degrees by means of one of a number of cogs in the camera's base that matched up to a huge cog on top of the tripod. It took a roll of film 25 cm wide and 240 cm long which was mounted in a magazine fitted to the camera's back. As the camera revolved one way, the film moved in the opposite direction across a vertical slit through which the exposure was made. A lever on the side of the magazine controlled the speed of rotation and movement and, with no shutter as such, this movement also governed exposure: the faster the rotation, the less exposure given; the slower the rotation, the more exposure.

The Cirkut was made right up until the 1940s and many are still doing the rounds today, used for taking those famous school photographs that call for a thousand boys to be arranged in a tiered semicircle while the camera, mounted on its tripod in the centre, scans the whole group.

Let's turn our attention once again to shutters, since by now, they were an all important part of camera design. Most camera makers used shutters made by separate specialist manufacturers and the most common design of the period we are discussing was the pneumatic shutter. In this, the exposure was determined by the movement of a tiny piston within a metal cylinder.

The Unicum pneumatic shutter.

In some, this meant that air leaked through a by-pass in the piston, while in others, the rate of movement was controlled by the amount of air allowed to leak out of the cylinder, and often the exposure was represented by the actual speed of the shutter blades' movement.

More common, however, was the method used in more sophisticated pneumatic shutters such as the Unicum where the blades always moved at the same speed. Exposure relied on the time that they were actually open and that was controlled by the variable length of the piston stroke within the cylinder.

The main fault with these mechanisms was the way working parts were exposed to the air, making them particularly susceptible to dust. The obvious next step was to put a case around the moving parts.

Perhaps the best known shutter of the early 20th Century was the Compound. It made its first appearance during the first years of the Century and in its improved and most popular form in 1909. The shutter was finished in black enamel and featured two levers, one for tensioning the shutter and the other for releasing it. The mechanism that worked the blades was totally enclosed and if a small cylinder was to be seen on the top, this was there only to facilitate the use of a pneumatic bulb release.

Up until this point, shutter blades were set alongside another set of blades that controlled the aperture; but in the Goerz and Volute shutters, one set of blades did both jobs: set f/8 at 1/25 sec and the blades would only open as far as that aperture during the exposure, set f/6.3 at 1 sec and the blades would open right up to *that* aperture for a second's exposure . . . and so on.

To write about shutters in any real detail could easily take up the rest of this book. So while no history of the camera could possibly be complete without a mention of the part they played, there is no room here to do the subject its full justice.

Back to cameras.

Despite its rising popularity, roll film was still an expensive luxury compared with plates, and alternatives that gave the best of both worlds were being explored. Cameras such as the Saint-Etienne Universelle of 1908 were made as plate cameras with provision for an easy-to-attach roll film back.

74

The Royal Mail camera.

On the novelty front, there was the Royal Mail camera made by W. Butcher and Son in 1908. In some ways, the camera was a throwback to the wet plate days; not in its choice of plates, but in the fact that it took fifteen exposures through as many lenses on one quarter-plate exposure. The resulting image fitted the portrait space on a postage stamp and special masks were available to give the finished print the look of a stamp with the chosen subject's face on it. Hence the name Royal Mail Camera.

But more than anything else, the time was right for a simple miniature, and for once, George Eastman was beaten to it. In 1909, the British firm of Houghton's Ltd. introduced the Ensignette, a collapsible bellows camera with a choice of meniscus or f/5.6 anastigmat lens.

Up until then, most miniature or vest pocket cameras had been made for plates or sheet film — the Goerz Tenax of 1908 for instance — so Houghton's made a big thing about the fact that the Ensignette was 'completely self-contained'. In other words, it took roll film, making a separate film or plate holder unnecessary.

Naturally, Eastman wasn't to be outdone for long and in 1912, he introduced the Vest Pocket Kodak, a folding design that measured no more than 12 x 6 x 2.5cm when folded and made to take 127 film.

Over the next few years, Eastman introduced two new additions to his basic cameras. The first in 1914, was an idea never tried before and never copied since — the autographic back. These specially designed camera backs were fitted to Folding Pocket and Vest Pocket Kodaks, and featured a small, rectangular trapdoor, together with a metal stylus. As each picture was taken, the photographer could snap open the trapdoor and, providing he was using special autographic film, write details of time, place, exposure, or anything else that appealed to him directly onto the film. When developed and printed in the normal way, the information would then be found written at the bottom of the print.

Eastman's second major addition to his cameras came in 1916 when his company issued their No 3A Autographic Special with a coupled rangefinder. It was the first of its type and remained the only coupled rangefinder camera on the market for the next twelve years.

There were three other types of camera that grew to fame during the period we are discussing here. One was the strut camera. These were bellows cameras in which the front panel was held rigid at a fixed distance from the film plane by four struts, one on each corner of the camera. Focusing was achieved by movement of the lens on its panel and sometimes by movement of the struts. For carrying, the struts were disengaged and folded into the body, followed by the lens panel. The Ensignette and Goerz Tenax already mentioned were strut cameras, as were many of their larger brothers made by firms like Zeiss and Ernemann.

The second style, like the first, also employed struts but the difference lay in the fact that they were criss-crossed like scissors and known as lazy tongs. The idea was pioneered by Arthur Newman who looked at the ordinary folding cameras of the day and decided the mechanisms employed were not good enough to hold the lens panel permanently rigid and parallel to the film plane. Thus was born the Sybil range of cameras that were to continue in popularity until well after the First World War in styles for roll film, film packs and plates.

The third style that really came into its own between 1900 and 1920 was the single lens reflex. The most popular design was that followed by cameras like the Auto-Graflex of 1907, the Premograph of 1908 or the Ica L'Artiste of 1910. They were essentially large boxes with a front panel that moved for focusing on bellows by means of a rack and pinion, and with a large hood that folded out of the top to shield the focusing screen. Because of the reflex principle involved, shutters were naturally focal plane types.

For every new camera, there was a new design, and yet there was still one design still very much in its embryonic stages during the years immediately prior to the First World War, but one which in due time would completely revolutionize the history of the camera.

In 1914, in Germany, a man named Oskar Barnack designed and built the prototype for a camera capable of taking 35mm cine film. It had an all metal body, a collapsible lens and focal plane shutter. The camera has gone down in photographic history as the original Leica.

The Sybil with lazy-tongs.

Thornton Pickard Victory Reflex.

7

The birth of 35 mm

Oskar Barnack was head of an experimental department in the German optical firm of Leitz, he was a keen amateur photographer and he enjoyed hiking; three factors which contributed to the birth of the Leica.

Tired of carrying a large plate camera with all its attendant paraphernalia on his hiking trips, Barnack was turning his thoughts to the possibility of a versatile miniature as early as 1905. In his attempts to produce a serious professional camera that could be hung round the neck or slipped into a pocket, he began his experiments by cutting down large glass plates and using them in a specially built miniature camera. But on enlargement, the course grain gave inferior results that were totally impractical.

It was later, while still working for Leitz, but this time on a motion picture camera, that the answer came to him. The 35 mm film used in these early movie cameras was obviously designed to produce the maximum sized enlargement from the minimum sized negative — after all, what better enlargement is there than a cinema screen? It was the breakthrough for which Barnack had been searching.

He built a miniature camera for use with 35 mm cine film and the result was the original Leica. That was in 1914; it was to be another nine years before the idea was further developed. In between came the First World War.

Just before the war, two significant companies were formed on the other side of the world. In 1917, an admiral in the Imperial Japanese Navy named Mitsubishi established a company called Nippon Kogaku (meaning *Japanese Optical Company*) for the purpose of supplying specialist optical and measuring equipment for military use. In 1919, also in Japan, the Asahi Optical Company was started as an eyeglass manufacturer.

At the time, neither company had any thoughts about cameras. But in time, both were to become famous for two of the best known names in single lens reflexes: Nikon and Asahi Pentax.

The First World War came and went and then, between

Above: the original Leica and (below) the Leica I of 1925.

79

1923 and 1924, thirty-one Leica cameras were hand-made and used to test public reaction. They had f/3.5 lenses, the focal plane shutters were calibrated, not in seconds, but in millimetres that represented the width of the slit in the blind and, for the first time in the history of the camera, a double exposure prevention device was built in.

The reaction from photographers and scientists alike was, in some cases, sceptical. But despite the fact that some took an instant dislike to the new miniature, Dr. Ernst Leitz decided to take the risk. The name Leica (derived from LEItz CAmera) was registered as a trademark and the camera went into production. The Leica I appeared on the market in 1925.

This first model, also known as the Model A, had an f/3.5 lens and shutter speeds from 1/5 to 1/500 sec. A year later, the Model B appeared, probably better known as the Compur Leica because of its Compur shutter which had taken the place of the Compound a few years before.

The Ica at full extension.

Lens interchangeability came with the Model C introduced in 1930, giving a choice between 35mm wide angle, 50mm standard and 135mm long focus lenses. And in 1932, the Leica II appeared with a rangefinder that coupled to a large assortment of lenses.

But already we are getting beyond ourselves. The Leica story with its many different models would fill a book on its own. So, having seen the camera on its way, let us return to earlier days.

The Leica, more than any other camera, popularized the start of 35mm photography, but it was by no means the first to use cine film for still pictures. Despite the fact that early movie film gave soot and whitewash effects, cameras were designed for its use almost as soon as the film itself appeared.

The Minigraph of 1915 was a good early example. It carried enough film for fifty exposures, each measuring 18 x 24 mm and sported an f/3.5 lens. The wooden-bodied Sico of 1922 had a Compur shutter and took twenty-five 30 x 40 mm exposures on paper-backed unperforated 35mm film. The Esco, made in Nuremberg in 1923 made a great play about the number of exposures it could take at one loading. Thanks to a couple of large round chambers on each side that dwarfed the camera itself, the Esco was capable of taking 400 pictures, each one measuring 18 x 24mm.

There was an unusual camera from France about this time. The Sept was made first in 1922 by Andre Debrie of Paris. It was advertised as a three-in-one camera because not

A film pack, seen here fitted to an Ica camera.

The Debrie Sept.

only could it take snapshots and time exposures, but with what can be considered as an early form of motor drive it could also be used as a movie camera. It took 35 mm film loaded into special cassettes and its main drawback was its single shutter speed. Exposure had to be varied by the aperture alone.

But the Sept was more than a camera (or more than three cameras if the advertising was to be believed). A panel opened in the back to allow the attachment of a light source which turned the camera into an enlarger or projector. Slots could also be opened top and bottom to feed through a roll of already developed negatives which then lay against the unexposed film. If the lens was then covered and the rear panel opened, contact printing to make positive pictures could be carried out actually within the camera.

One of the biggest advances in the 1920s was in lenses. Wider and wider apertures were appearing all the time and in 1924, the Ermanox was introduced, sporting the previously unheard of top aperture of f/2.

The Ermanox was designed for single exposures on 4.5 x 6 cm plates and rapidly became popular as the first truly candid camera. It measured only 7 x 9 x 11.25cm and was sold with the slogan, *What you see, you can photograph*. A year before the Leica I, it revolutionized available light photography.

We are dealing here with an age when films and plates went side by side. While cameras like the Leica were extolling the virtues of roll film, the smaller the better; other makers like Sanderson were steadfast in their thinking towards plates. A glance at a Wallace Heaton advert of 1923 shows far more plate cameras for sale than roll film models and yet, you can almost see the niggling doubt in the minds of the plate camera manufacturers. They thought they were right to go on producing their models, but just supposing roll film did win the day . . . what then?

It was this thinking that led to the growing popularity of film packs. A flat box containing the pack fitted the back of a plate camera in place of the usual plate holder. The pack contained perhaps a dozen sheets of cut film. Each sheet was attached to a tab of paper which was numbered and protruded from the top of the pack. As an exposure was taken, the first of the tabs was pulled and the film attached was rolled away from the film plane and round to the back of the pack, leaving the next sheet ready for the following exposure.

Plate cameras of course, were still being made to take roll film backs as well, but strange as it may seem, even the roll film makers didn't seem too sure of themselves. In their hearts, they still saw that plates gave superior results and so they took out their own form of insurance. Which is why some roll film cameras appeared with a provision for plates.

The Ensign Regular was a perfect example. On the surface, it looked like a perfectly ordinary 120 size roll film camera modelled on similar lines to the Folding Pocket Kodak. But closer examination of the camera's back, would

Three examples of how cameras were sometimes made for either film or plates. Left to right: Eastman No. 4, Series C quarter plate camera with film back; Ensign Regular folding camera with plate back and Brevete with film back.

have revealed a small lever that allowed a thin metal flap to be slid aside, revealing a facility for taking 8.5 x 6cm plates.

But roll film *was* catching on, gradually taking over more and more plate camera strongholds. The bulky single lens reflex that had been popular since the 1880s and which had held onto its plate design beginnings for years, suddenly began to appear in roll film form. Cameras like the Ensign Roll Film Reflex of 1922 for eight exposures on 120 film, a simple model shaped like a box camera laid horizontally but with a reflex mirror which threw its image onto a ground-glass screen in the camera's top. The screen was shielded by a tall hood twice the height of the actual camera and which folded onto the top when not in use.

A tropical version of the Ensign Roll Film Reflex.

How one thing led to another. The Heidoscope (left) and first model Rolleiflex.

One interesting point about this model was the fact that it didn't use the focal plane shutter that was normally necessary in a single lens reflex camera to prevent light from the lens and viewfinder from leaking onto the film. Here's how it worked:-

At the start, the mirror would be flush with the inside of the focusing screen, blocking any light from fogging the film. The movement of a lever on the top of the camera then brought the mirror down to its normal 45 degree angle while, at the same time, opening the shutter behind the lens. The mirror now not only reflected its image up to the ground-glass screen, but also made an effective trap within the body that prevented light from the open shutter from reaching the film.

When the picture had been composed, one of two buttons was pressed on the front of the camera. The mirror flipped up and the shutter snapped shut, all in the fraction of a second needed to make the exposure.

The Ensign Roll Film Reflex wasn't the first of the front

shutter reflexes because Newman and Guardia were playing with the same idea back in 1902, but it is an interesting example of a design which, in the end, proved too complex for its own good.

In 1928, there was another major advance in camera design with the introduction of the first truly compact twin lens reflex. To trace its origins, however, we must go back briefly to 1920 when a firm called Franke and Heidecke was started, initially with a view to the stereo camera market. Their first production was the Heidoscope, a stereo plate camera with reflex viewfinder. It had three lenses, two for taking and one in the middle that projected its image onto a ground-glass screen.

Then, in 1923, the company produced a roll film version of the Heidoscope called the Rolleidescope and, looking at it, you can almost see the reasoning that led to their next design: take one lens away, turn the camera on its end and put the ground-glass screen on the top. The result was the first Rolleiflex.

The first model in 1928 took 117 film, the same size as 120 but giving only six 6 x 6cm square exposures. The camera had a rim-set Compur shutter speeded from 1 to 1/300 sec and an f/4.5 Tessar lens. Film transport was by the traditional knob and red window method.

The Baby Rollei which first appeared in 1931, took 127 film, giving twelve 4 x 4cm pictures on a roll. But because 127 film was only numbered from one to eight, a new method of automatic counting was needed. So the Baby Rollei appeared with crank winding. The usual red window was used to bring the first number into view and thereafter, the correct amount of film was advanced each time the handle was cranked.

Crank winding subsequently became a standard feature of the Rolleiflex and was introduced to the larger 6 x 6cm format a year later when the third model was introduced for 120 film.

Exakta B.

Up until the advent of the Rolleiflex, all reflex cameras, both single and twin lens, had been bulky affairs and twin lens models, by virtue of their extra lens, had always been the more cumbersome of the two designs. Now suddenly the tables were turned. The twin lens reflex had been transformed from a bulky giant into a compact masterpiece, leaving its single lens cousin looking like an ungainly monster.

Clearly, something had to be done about it, and in 1933, the first truly compact roll film single lens reflex came onto the market. The camera was the Exakta.

Produced by Ihagee in Dresden, the Exakta used 127 film. It sported an f/2.8 lens and a focal plane shutter speeded from 1/25 to 1/1000 sec. The Model B that followed took the shutter speeds down to a full 12 seconds, had a built-in self-timer and was synchronised for flash.

Then, in 1936, Ihagee brought out a 35mm model. It was called the Kine Exakta and it set the style for one of the most popular designs of camera ever produced — the 35mm single lens reflex.

Kine Exakta.

8

The clever, the compact and the complicated

The Ensign Cupid of 1922. First sixteen-on camera.

The 1930s were a time of tremendous innovation. Between 1930 and 1940, every year seemed to see the emergence of a major name in the history of the camera. It was the age of the miniature, a time when cameras became compact, clever and complicated — and some became too complicated for their own good.

The final breakthrough for colour film came in the 1930s. Although colour photography both on plates and film had been around for a quarter of a century, every other process was finally put in the shade by the arrival of the integral tripack made possible with Kodachrome in 1935.

Destined to become the first commercially successful amateur colour film, this was a reversal material invented by Leopold Mannes and Leopold Godowsky in co-operation with the Kodak research laboratories. Kodachrome first appeared in 16mm size for movie films; 35mm for still cameras arrived in 1936, the year Agfa brought out their own brand of colour film called Agfacolor.

It would be easy to fill the rest of this book with details of the various experiments that led up to the final production of a viable colour film; just as it would be easy to write a lot more about how colour films progressed after 1935. But the aim of this book is to write about cameras rather than processes; so having noted that it was now easy to take colour film in everyday cameras, let us return to the subject in hand.

It was black and white film, rather than colour film that affected camera design in the 1930s and, with the advent of Kodak's Verichrome and Ilford's Selochrome, films at last began to do justice to lenses. With better quality negatives, camera manufacturers turned their attention to getting smaller and therefore more pictures from every roll of film.

So it was that roll film cameras with their maximum of twelve pictures per roll set out to challenge the economies of 35mm. The result was a new craze for sixteen-on cameras,

Zeiss Ikon Box Tengor. At only 8cm high, it was one of the smallest box cameras ever made.

Part of Kodak's first English camera works at Harrow where many of the company's famous names of the 1930s were designed and built. The collection of buildings became known as 'Tin Town'.

models designed to take sixteen pictures on a roll of 120 or 127 film by taking the eight-on format and cutting it in half.

The idea began with the launch of an Ensign film with the letter X marked between each number that enabled the user to stop winding half way between frames. Used in conjunction with a special mask fitted into the film plane, certain cameras could be converted to take sixteen exposures to a roll.

The first camera specifically designed for the sixteen-on format was the strange little Ensign Cupid of 1922 but it was in the 1930s as a direct challenge to 35mm that the style really caught on. By then, special film was replaced by the more practical idea of using standard film in a camera with two red windows in place of the usual one.

The idea was that for sixteen-on pictures, the figure 1 was wound into the first window and then, after exposure, it was wound into the second window. For the third picture, figure 2 was wound into the first window and so on right through the roll. Very often, the camera was supplied with a detachable mask for sixteen-on which, when removed, gave the usual eight-on by using only one window.

A perfect example was the Kolibri made by Zeiss Ikon in 1930. At a time when vest pocket cameras were giving way to 35mm, the Kolibri was the perfect compromise. It looked like a vest pocket model but, loaded with 127 film, it gave sixteen exposures, 3 x 4cm to a roll. Even so, the Kolibri was fighting a losing battle and lasted only a couple of years.

The first Contax.

Kodak set their sights on Boy Scouts and Girl Guides in 1931 when they introduced two new versions of their Vest Pocket Kodaks for these two organisations. The company were licensed to incorporate the Boy Scout and Girl Guide emblems into the cameras which were made in blue for the girls and green for the boys. These were the first Kodak cameras sold complete with carrying case and were made to hook onto a Scout or Guide belt.

The following year, in 1932, Kodak acquired the camera works at Stuttgart from Dr. August Nagel and straightaway, his brother Hugo came to England to set up a design and development team at Harrow. It was this team that was responsible for turning out many of Kodak's successful designs of the 1930s including a six-20 folding camera and, in 1934, the most advanced version to date of the Brownie, a model for 620 film with f/11 doublet lens, two supplementary lenses and three stops.

The Baby Brownie.

By 1939, design had been completed for an all-metal range of box cameras but production was interrupted by the Second World War and these Six-20 Brownies were eventually the first cameras to roll off the Kodak production lines straight after the war. Between 1946 and 1959, 9,000,000 were made at Harrow.

But we are getting beyond ourselves. Back in 1932, Zeiss Ikon, previously renowned for their plate and roll film cameras, surrendered at last to the popularity of 35mm. The result was the first Contax which appeared in the same year, and in competition to, the Leica II. The two cameras were similar in many ways. Both took 35mm film, both had coupled rangefinders.

But the Contax was a long way from being little more than a copy of its contemporary. It was a very individual camera with some very individual design ideas, not least of which was its slightly out of the ordinary shutter. It moved vertically instead of horizontally and was made up from a series of metal slats like a roll-top desk.

The first Super Ikontas appeared from Zeiss in 1933. They were folding cameras for 8 x 6cm pictures that sprung open to the taking position at the touch of a button and which used a unique form of coupled rangefinder. Such an accessory was, of course, not unknown before the Super Ikonta; and rangefinders were already being coupled to lenses in the current miniatures, but the Super Ikonta was the first since the Kodak model to make the idea popular on roll film cameras.

Most rangefinders of that time worked by looking at the subject from two viewpoints, thus giving two images which were brought together by a tilting mirror. When the images

Below: the Super Ikonta with its unique rangefinder. Right: Zeis Ikon's Ikoflex (left) and the Voigtlander Brilliant.

Three miniatures of the 1930s. Left to right: the Ensign Midget, an Eljy made by Lumiere and a Coronet Vogue.

The Kodak Retina.

Two sub-miniatures: the Merlin . . .

coincided, the distance was read off a dial. Zeiss tackled the idea differently.

They mounted a tiny glass window beside the lens. Inside this, were two wedges of glass, layed with the thin end of one against the thick end of the other, so that the result was a parallel-sided piece of flat glass which in no way changed the direction of light passing through it. As the front element of the Super Ikonta's lens was revolved for focusing, so these two wedges also revolved, one in the opposite direction to the other. After 180 degrees of turning, the wedges would end up thick end against thick and thin against thin, giving a prism of glass which, unlike the flat version, *did* change the light's direction.

It can be seen therefore, that revolving these two wedges changed the direction of the light through the glass at varying angles and giving a perfect way of swinging one of the sighting lines in a rangefinder. Optically, the result was far superior to the tilting mirror in most other rangefinders and as the instrument was coupled directly to the front element of the camera lens, the Super Ikonta ended up with one of the most superior rangefinders yet seen.

There were new models with unique designs appearing on the market all through the 1930s, but there were new variations on old designs as well. The Voigtlander Prominent, also born in 1933 was such a camera. Basically, it was a folder that sprang open at the touch of a button and which took either eight or sixteen pictures on 120 film. But the manufacturers added so many bits and pieces that it took on a weird and wonderful shape never before seen in the style.

It featured a special light-tight series of openings in the bellows for letting air in and out as the camera was opened or closed, an f/4.5 lens, shutter speeded from 1 - 1/250 sec, coupled rangefinder and extinction type built-in exposure meter. The extra accessories not normally associated with a humble folder added knobs and dials to the bodywork, giving it an ugly appearance that probably accounted more than anything else for its unexpected lack of popularity.

The camera died, but the name lived on, and in the years that followed the Second World War, Voigtlander produced their second version of the Prominent, this time, a 35mm non-reflex model with interchangeable lenses.

But the folding camera wasn't the only design that ran through several different makes. The Rolleiflex was now beginning to show its influence over other manufacturers.

... and the Coronet Midget

In 1933, Voigtlander introduced the Superb, a twin lens reflex with a unique parallax correction device achieved by actually tilting the viewing lens and screen within the camera so that each of the twin lenses always aimed at the exact point of focus. Ironically, the Superb didn't do as well as the Brilliant, a cheaper Voigtlander with the appearance of a twin lens reflex but whose viewing screen was really nothing more than a big condenser lens type viewfinder.

The Ikoflex was another twin lens reflex that came out of the Zeiss works in 1934. The first models had lateral film transport operated by a lever wind at the camera's base, but this gave way on later models to vertical transport by the more usual winding knob.

And in 1935 the Rollei works copied their own design to give us the Rolleiflex's cheap cousin, the Rolleicord. It was a

A Voigtlander Bessa. The shutter release on this model was under the baseboard.

Two sixteen-on cameras: the Kodak Duo 620 (left) and an Ensign Autorange.

Two 35mm cameras from the 1930s: The Certo Dollina (right) and — showing a strong influence from Kodak's Retina — a small Balda.

94

Quarter-plate Sandersons like this model were on sale until 1939.

basic twin lens reflex with film transport supplied by turning a knob and operating a counting mechanism. With a simple Triotar lens, the Rolleicord sold for about half the price of a Rolleiflex.

Not that these medium format cameras came anywhere near killing off the interest in miniaturization. The interest was there all right but by now it had become apparent that in some ways, 35mm cameras were defeating their own object. While the film was more economical than standard roll film, the cameras that used it were too expensive for the average amateur to even think about buying. What was needed was a well made, quality 35mm camera that would sell for a fraction of the cost of a Contax or Leica.

As was so often the case, it was Kodak who came up with

Above: the Contaflex, an unusual 35mm twin lens reflex.

Top: the Kwanon, soon to become Canon. Left: the Reflex Korelle, first 6 × 6 cm single lens reflex.

the answer by launching, in 1934, the first of the Retinas, a folding camera for 35mm with an f/3.5 lens specially designed for the format by Schneider and a Compur shutter speeded to 1/300 sec. It was quality coupled with cheapness that made the Retina series, probably more than any other, responsible for the real popularization of 35mm photography.

But the 35mm format didn't necessarily rely on 35mm film. The same year also saw the birth of the Ensign Midget, an interesting little strut camera measuring no more than 9 x 4 x 1.5cm when closed. It came at first in two models, one with a fixed focus lens and the other with an f/6.3 Ensar and shutter speeded from 1/25 to 1/100 sec. The camera took six pictures on special Ensign film known as E10 and the negative size of 30 x 40mm was only slightly larger than the conventional 35mm format.

Several of these roll film miniatures appeared over the next few years. The Coronet Vogue was a fixed focus, fixed aperture, single shutter speed model made of bakelite and designed for use with 'Vogue V35' film. The camera measured 11 x 7.5 x 2.5cm when folded and the picture size was 50 x 30mm.

Smaller still was the Coronet Midget that appeared in 1936 for 16mm roll film. Picture size in this was a mere 18 x 12mm from a camera that measured only 6 x 2.5 x 3cm.

And 1937 saw the Eljy from the French firm of Lumiere. This was a rigid bodied camera measuring 8 x 4.5 x 4cm that featured an f/3.5 lens, a shutter speeded from 1/25 to 1/125 sec and which gave negatives 36 x 24mm, the standard 35mm format, on unperforated film.

The mid-1930s also saw a strange hybrid of the miniature and the medium format worlds; a 35mm twin lens reflex considered by many to be the pinnacle of perfection both then and for many years to come. It arrived in 1935 and was produced by Zeiss who saw it as being two cameras in one — a reflex and a Contax. Consequently, they called it the Contaflex (not to be confused with the single lens reflex of the same name produced by Zeiss after the Second World War).

The Contaflex, like a few other early twin lens reflexes, featured horizontal film transport across the camera body but, unlike any other, it produced a standard 36 x 24mm negative on 35mm film. While this size was suitable for a negative, however, the manufacturers were swift to realize that it was far too small for accurate focusing. So the Contaflex became the only camera to have a viewing screen with a larger image than the negative area.

This was achieved by using lenses of different focal lengths for taking and viewing. The taking lens was a 50mm focal length in a choice of f/2.8, f/2 or f/1.5. The viewing lens was a longer focal length with the extra light path accommodated by placing the reflex mirror as far back as possible and then moving the viewing screen an appropriate amount higher than usual. The effect was to give the Contaflex a tall, slim look never seen before or since in a twin lens reflex.

There was a range of interchangeable lenses — all of which coupled with the viewing lens when the screen was masked down proportionally and this screen not only had a brilliancy condenser fitted, it also sported a hinged magnifier inside the hood for critical focusing.

As if this wasn't enough, the camera had a built-in exposure meter, equipped with a series of prisms that changed the angle of the sensitive cell's view along with the lens, a metal focal plane shutter speeded from ½ to 1/1000 sec and a delayed action feature.

The Contaflex was ahead of its time. It was a camera equipped to produce the best ever results on 35mm film. Unfortunately the film at that time wasn't up to handling those results. The format was still considered a bit of a novelty in some areas and its grain structure was nowhere near as fine as present standards.

Stereo photography, while no longer as popular as it had been at the beginning of the Century, still hovered under the surface of camera manufacture, rearing its head now and then with an unusual model of twin lens camera. In 1935, no less a manufacturer than Leitz considered the possibilities of such a camera with a prototype stereo Leica.

This prototype was made personally by Oskar Barnack and was designed as two cameras in one with a double shutter. Height and width of the camera were the same as a standard model but the length of the camera was 19.3cm, housing two lens flanges 7cm apart. The size of each stereo frame was 24 x 22.5mm and after each exposure, the film was advanced the equivalent of two frames.

The stereo Leica, however, remained only a prototype and was never actually put into production, even though the company did make several attachments to convert standard models to stereo photography.

Meanwhile, half way across the world . . .

Things were beginning to stir now in the Japanese camera industry. Nippon Kogaku who, for the previous eighteen years, had made only military optical and measuring equipment, turned their attention in 1935 to producing their first

98

The complicated Compass.

The Welta Perfekta. A twin lens reflex whose unusual feature was a focusing screen that could be turned sideways for horizontal pictures.

camera. Both the camera and explicit details have been lost. All that is known of what in essence was the first Nikon, is that it was a 35 mm rangefinder camera with an interchangeable 50mm f/2 lens.

A second Japanese company established two years earlier in nothing more than a rented three-room apartment in Tokyo, also produced a camera that year; but the genesis of their model lay in an event of six years before. It was in 1929 that the Graf Zeppelin made a stopover in Tokyo. The skipper had a Leica — the first to be seen in Japan and a style that was soon blatantly copied by that small three-room company whose name was The Precision Instruments Optical Research Laboratory.

The camera, which inevitably bore an uncanny resemblance to the Leica, was the first domestic Japanese camera with a focal plane shutter. It was called the Kwanon after the Buddhist Goddess of Mercy, but when the religious connotations subsequently proved unacceptable, the company changed the name to Canon.

The following year, 1936, saw the arrival of the first 6 x 6cm single lens reflex. The Reflex-Korelle sported an f/3.5 Schneider-Kreuznach lens and focal plane shutter speeded from 1/10 to 1/1000 sec. The camera was sold again after the Second World War as the Agiflex.

The same year also saw the introduction of an unusual little camera called the Perma. With an f/6.3 fixed focus, fixed aperture lens, the camera had three shutter speeds controlled, strangely enough, by the way it was held. Horizontal, it gave 1/50 sec, but if the photographer turned the camera on its side he would hear a quiet click that indicated that the shutter would now operate at 1/25 sec. Held on its opposite side, the speed increased to 1/450 sec. The device was known as a gravity shutter and the pictures produced were naturally square — sixteen on 127 film.

At the beginning of this chapter we mentioned that some of the cameras that appeared in the 1930s were too complicated for their own good. A perfect example came in 1936 from a Swiss watch and clock manufacturer called Lecoultre. The camera was the Compass, an intricately beautiful masterpiece of miniature engineering that in many ways was doomed from the start. Consider first its specification:-

An f/3.5 lens with rotary shutter in twenty-two speeds from 1/500 to four-and-a-half full seconds. A rangefinder in a separate window to the viewfinder which, in turn, had a pivoting mirror for right-angle viewing. A metal body, incorporating a device for taking stereo or panoramic pictures. Built-in yellow, green and orange filters. A ground-glass screen with focusing magnifier. Collapsible lens hood, hinged lens cap and built-in spirit level. Built-in exposure meter and depth of field scale. It took single pictures on plates or cut film and also had a roll film back.

Now you know its specification, take a look at its size: folded, the camera measured no more than 7 x 7 x 3cm.

The Compass was probably one of the most beautiful little cameras that has ever been produced. Unfortunately, the very nature of its beauty was its downfall. Put its specification on a camera five times the size and you have an extremely worthy piece of equipment. Put the same specification on a miniature and all those accessories and controls are just too fiddly. Their size made the photographer feel like a clumsy oaf and, with the outbreak of the Second World War, the Compass died away, never to be seen again.

A miniature that did survive, however, was the Minox,

The Minox, one of the few really successful sub-miniatures.

made by Valsts Electro-Techniska Fabrika in Latvia and seen for the first time in 1937. The Minox rapidly became epitomized as the ideal spy camera, a role which it continues to hold today if television and films are anything to go by. It was a perfect example of the really practical miniature, taking fifty 8 x 11mm pictures on 9.5mm unperforated film, loaded into special cassettes, all housed in a slender body measuring 1 x 2 x 8cm. The lens unusually, had a fixed aperture of f/3.5 with the exposure controlled by shutter speeds ranging from ½ to 1/1000 sec. The shutter was cocked and the film advanced each time the camera was slid closed and opened again.

The first camera to feature automatic exposure control appeared in 1938 and with an already impressive track record, it isn't difficult to guess the maker. Once again, Kodak was first in the field.

The camera was the Super Kodak Six-20, a folding bellows camera for eight exposures on 620 film. It had a shutter speeded from 1 to 1/200 sec, coupled rangefinder and apertures from f/3.5 to f/22 that were varied automatically according to the light being read by a photo cell spread across the camera's width above the lens.

Kodak's brief had always been to make photography simple while bringing advanced techniques within the range of the man in the street. With the Super Kodak Six-20, they again proved their point. For the first time, Mr. Average could buy a camera that was technically competent of producing worthwhile results under varying conditions but which, unlike its predecessors, assured the photographic layman of a correctly exposed negative every time.

The Super Kodak Six-20, the first automatic camera.

9

Instant pictures

As the Second World War ended, production lines at Kodak swung into action with the Brownie Model C.

It started with a father taking pictures of his young daughter; it ended with a giant step in the history of the camera. The father was Dr. Edwin Land and his daughter, having had her photograph taken, became upset when she learned how long she would have to wait to see the results. The little girl's impatience led her father to begin wondering

about the possibility of building a camera that not only took a picture, but also developed it instantly within a minute of the exposure being made. The result was the first Polaroid camera and the rest is history.

Dr. Land announced his instant picture process at a meeting of the Optical Society of America in 1947 and the first firm he approached with a view to turning the system into a commercial proposition turned the idea down flat. It was nothing more than a gimmick, they said, and one without a future. In 1948, the first instant picture camera appeared on the market. Fourteen years later, 14,000,000 had been sold and the Polaroid Land Corporation was the second largest producer of photographic materials in America.

Land's first instant picture camera was known as the Model 95. It was a folding design but somewhat larger than the majority of roll film cameras of that time. It had an f/11 lens and exposure was simplified by coupling the aperture to the shutter speeds, giving a range of combinations from 1/8 sec at f/11 to 1/60 sec at f/45.

Instant pictures were achieved by use of Polaroid Land film which consisted of a negative emulsion and positive paper on two separate rolls, together with pods of chemicals. As each picture was taken, the photographer pulled a tab which led the exposed negative, the positive paper and a chemical pod through two tight rollers. The pod broke and released the chemical which was spread evenly between the negative and positive sandwich.

It was this chemical, rather than light as would have been the normal practice, that transferred the image from one to the other. The positive image was formed on the paper with the help of the unexposed silver crystals from the negative.

The pictures were sepia, but in 1950, a new black and white orthochromatic film called Type 41 was introduced. Two years later, the first instant camera for professional use appeared on the market. It was the Model 110 with an f/4.5 lens and shutter speeds of up to 1/500 sec.

Polaroid went on extending their range right throughout the 1950s, and in 1958, they took their process a step further by producing separate Polaroid backs to fit conventional cameras. The back consisted of a holder that took film packets with the negative-positive sandwich and processing pods enclosed within a light-tight envelope. For processing, the envelope was pulled through the usual rollers and all the way out of the holder, where it continued developing inside the black envelope.

The Polaroid Model 95, the first instant picture camera.

The Polaroid story is one that has never stood still and, as we shall see later, they went on to develop more and more sophisticated forms of instant photography which in 1963 inevitably led to instant colour. Of which, more later.

The late 1940s and early 1950s have, however, gone down in the history of the camera for more than the birth of instant photography. The first eye-level, single lens reflex appeared in 1948. With the Contax S — the first miniature with a pentaprism — the photographer could hold the camera to his eye and see exactly what he was photographing, the right way round and the right way up. The camera also differed from previous Contax models by replacing the old metal focal plane shutter with one of cloth and by changing the lens mount from bayonet to screw fitting. The Swedish Hasselblad 1600F was introduced the same year. Two cameras, both single lens reflexes, one for 35mm, the other for 6 x 6cm; between them, they revolutionised their respective formats.

Stereo cameras enjoyed a brief revival in the 1950s with models like the Iloca Rapid that had f/2.8 lenses, Stereo Pronto SVS shutter speeded from 1 to 1/300 sec and a

Ensign Commando. Its unusual feature was a rangefinder coupled to a moving film plane, rather than the lens.

The Contax S, first single lens reflex with a pentaprism.

coupled rangefinder. Slightly more unusual from the early 1950s, was the Italian Iso Duplex which used 120 film widthwise, giving two images 24 x 24mm square across the film. The lenses were f/6.3 and shutters were speeded from 1/25 to 1/100 sec.

But, as had so often been the case before, the stereo craze was brief and soon died, even though the Russians brought out a plastic model as late as 1960. It was called the Sputnik and had not two lenses, but three; the two outside lenses for the stereo pair and the one in the middle and slightly above the other two for a ground-glass screen. All three were geared together for focusing.

In 1952, after seven years of research, the first 35mm single lens reflex came out of Japan. But despite the influence of the eye-level Contax, it stuck to the rather more tried and tested formula of the waist-level viewfinder. The camera was the Asahiflex, made by the Asahi Optical Company. It had a 50mm f/3.5 Takumar lens and a focal plane shutter speeded from 1/25 to 1/500 sec. As well as its waist-level viewfinder, it also featured an eye-level optical viewfinder, though this of course was not reflex.

Two years later, Asahi scored their own first. Up until then, all single lens reflexes had suffered a common fault: the picture in the viewfinder blacked out after the exposure

107

had been made as the mirror flipped out of the light path and
failed to return until it was physically lowered into position
— usually by a mechanism coupled to film wind and shutter
tensioning. In 1954, the Asahiflex II appeared with the
world's first instant return mirror, an invention of the Asahi
Optical Company.

Three years after that, the company designed their first
camera with a built-in pentaprism and named it after a
corruption of the two words *pentaprism* and *Asahiflex*. The
result was the first Pentax.

The span of years between 1948 and 1957 was also
important for another Japanese camera manufacturer.
Nippon Kogaku released the Nikon I in 1948. In appearance and specification, it was just about identical to the pre-
war Zeiss Contax, a fact that the then current open house on
patents made perfectly permissible.

It was probably the Korean War more than any other
factor that made Japanese cameras in general and Nikons in
particular known to the western world. By 1952, the Far East
was crawling with western newsmen covering the war and,
finding no repair facilities for their Leicas and Contaxes in
the East, they turned to the locally produced goods. It

wasn't long before they realized they were on to a good thing.

By the end of 1956, the Nikon S rangefinder models were in wide use, offering a choice of over thirty lenses from 25mm to 350mm and with a 50mm standard lens that featured the previously unheard of wide open aperture of f/1. There was also available an equally revolutionary motor drive that gave the user the benefit of four frames per second shooting.

Nikon was probably one of the first companies to recognise the importance of being able to shoot at several frames per second with a camera, so much so that when they introduced their first single lens reflex in 1957, it was designed right from the start to accept motor drive. It was this model, more than any other, that made Nikon a household name with professional photographers world-wide. The camera was the Nikon F. It lacked a metering system of course in those days, but a Photomic viewfinder could be attached which sported its own photo electric cell linked to the shutter and diaphragm.

But while the precision miniatures were growing more professional every day, there was, as always, a strong market for the casual snapshotters, and for them box cameras were still the order of the day. Even in the mid-1950s, Kodak were still launching new models. Their Six-20 Brownie Model F was about as sophisticated as any simple box camera could ever hope to be.

The camera was finished in a buff leather cloth with a brown metal front plate. Large, clear viewfinders were surrounded by frames of polished brass, while both the shutter release and film wind knob were of white plastic. Aperture and focus were fixed but the shutter could be

110

moved from instantaneous to brief time at the flick of a lever. There was a supplementary lens built in for subjects closer than ten feet and a built-in yellow filter as well as facilities for cable release and flashgun.

But by then, it must have been clear that the box camera was finally on the way out as simple cameras began taking on shapes never before seen. The Ensign Ful-Vue Super for instance. If current advertisements are to be believed, the original Ful-Vue 'revolutionised photography in 1939' and with the Super version released in 1955, the advertisers were ready to claim: 'The Ful-Vue Super looks and performs like an expensive twin lens reflex.'

Well true it did look a little like a twin lens reflex, having two lenses mounted on the front. But the top lens was there only to provide an image for the extra large viewfinder. Its unusual shape was quite streamlined but its specification of a single speed shutter and fixed aperture made it really no more than a box camera with a super viewfinder. True the lens could be focused from two metres to infinity, but the focusing movement was in no way coupled to the viewing lens and it would have taken a good stretch of the imagination to compare the camera with a real twin lens reflex such as the Rolleiflex.

Even cameras that were *called* box cameras were beginning to stray away from the traditional shape. The Ilford Envoy Box Camera was synchronised for flash and had a direct vision viewfinder.

A similar style was seen in the Agfa Clack that sported two apertures, a built-in portrait lens and a choice of instantaneous or brief time exposures, as well as flash synchronisation; or in the equally similar Kodak Six-20 Brownie Special.

It was at this time that Kodak, as ever with their eye on the snapshooting man in the street, introduced a camera that more than any other hammered home the last nail in the box camera's coffin. The camera was the Kodak Brownie 127.

Smart and inexpensive, with an eye-level optical viewfinder, single speed shutter and fixed focus, fixed aperture, meniscus lens, it was one of the least sophisticated cameras around. Yet its ease of operation was surpassed only by its popularity. Suddenly, box cameras that had been in the family for years were relegated to the loft as snapshotters everywhere began buying the Brownie 127.

The 1950s were a time of change, but they were also a time when many old styles lingered on. At the beginning of the decade, plates and film packs were rife; by the end, the 35mm single lens reflex had established itself as the professional tool. And yet, in 1955, there were still manufacturers turning out brass and mahogany plate cameras with separate shutters which could easily have passed for models from the turn of the century.

The Aptus is a case in point. Looking at such a camera now, who would believe that it came from the same decade as the Nikon F? Made by Moore and Company of Liverpool, the Aptus had been around from as far back as 1895, when it was used for ferrotype photography. But the latest version that was being made and sold in 1955 operated on a new system that worked like this:-

Anything up to 100 sheets of a special sensitive material on an aluminium foil base were loaded into a magazine in the base of the camera. These were taken out one at a time and held in the film plane by a weird and wonderful suction-operated holder. Once the exposure had been made, the sheet was dropped straight down into a special developing tank clamped on the base of the camera. Once development was completed, the tank was swivelled through 180 degrees and the developed sheet removed to be fixed in a separate tank.

The operator now had a negative which he slotted into a copying arm that incorporated a supplementary lens and the whole thing was mounted on the front of the camera. The negative was copied and thus the new negative, when developed in the same way, became the finished positive.

In 1957, Kodak took their simple cameras another step forward and introduced the Brownie Star series, the first low-priced cameras designed specifically to take colour slides as well as colour and monochrome prints. One of the series, the Kodak Brownie Starflash, became the first Kodak camera to feature a built-in flashgun. By 1962, Kodak had sold more than 10,000,000 Brownie Stars, but by then they were already thinking of a new type of camera, one that would once again prove their ability to be first in the field with revolutionary new styles.

A year later, the first Kodak Instamatic appeared and a new era in cameras was born.

The Ensign Ful-Vue Super (right) with the original Ful-Vue.

The changing face of box cameras. Left to right: Nustyle de Luxe, Coronet Twelve-20, Ensign Ful-Vue and Six-20 Brownie Special.

The highly popular Kodak Brownie 127.

10

The electronic age

Three major innovations epitomize the 1960s: electronics, automation and mass production.

Between 1959 and 1961, the history of the camera took two giant steps forward at the Canon plant in Japan with the introduction of the Model P and Canonet. Up until the Model P, camera manufacture was a job for experts and good quality equipment was made by hand, one camera at a time. But at Canon, camera making was getting a new look. Production was streamlined, parts standardized and for the first time a conveyor belt appeared in the workrooms. The Model P was the world's first high-quality camera to be mass produced on an assembly line.

Price was the breakthrough which made the Canonet so remarkable. It was launched at the 1960 Photokina as a good quality camera which could be bought with one month's salary — a good deal less than comparable cameras of the day. The Canonet was a 35mm model with coupled range-finder, but the thing that set it apart and gave it a unique look was the design of the meter cell which circled the lens, giving an automatic correction for filters which fitted over the whole assembly.

This first entry by Canon into the popular market received so much publicity that buyers are reputed to have literally fought at sales counters to buy the camera when it went on sale a year later.

This first appearance by Canon at Photokina also launched a remarkable new lens made by the company. The focal length was a standard 50mm, but the aperture was an astounding f/0.95 — more sensitive even than the human eye, if advertisements of the time are to be believed.

In the same year at Polaroid, Dr. Edwin Land gave a progress demonstration of instant colour at the annual shareholders' meeting, taking three pictures in one of the company's regular cameras. It was another three years before his instant colour film went on worldwide sale. Also in 1960, Polaroid announced the Model 900 Electric Eye Camera, its first fully automatic model and development

The Mec 16 SB. An early camera with through the lens metering.

The Topcon RE Super, the first single lens reflex with through-the-lens metering.

114

The first Kodak Instamatic for 126 size cartridges.

time of instant black and white pictures was cut from one minute right back to between ten and fifteen seconds.

Japan was the next country with a significant landmark in the history of the camera. It came in 1962 in the shape of the Topcon RE Super, the camera usually credited with being the first model with through-the-lens metering. What isn't generally known is that the Topcon RE Super was predated by at least two years by another through-the-lens metering camera, a 16mm sub-miniature made by Feinwerketechnik of Germany. The Mec 16 SB sold in England in 1960 and utilized a Selenium cell behind the lens; a fact that the instruction book was swift to point out meant no more worries over filter factors as the meter took its readings through both lens *and* any filter which might be attached.

The Mec, of course, was a non-reflex camera and, in all

The Canon Pellix, a single lens reflex without the traditional moving mirror.

The Mycro IIIA, a Japanese sub-miniature that took 14mm roll film, pictured here against a standard 35mm cassette.

fairness to the Topcon company, it was their RE Super, a top quality 35mm single lens reflex, that brought through-the-lens metering to the attention of the world and set a style that was rapidly followed by just about every other major manufacturer.

By now, of course, the 35mm single lens reflex had been accepted by professionals and serious amateurs as the ideal camera for compactness, convenience and versatility. But that still left one very large section of the camera-buying public who would never have the need for such sophistication. The time was again ripe for something revolutionary in the snapshooting market and, as usual, it was Kodak who supplied it in 1963 with the first Kodak Instamatic.

In this, film loading was greatly simplified by the introduction of a pre-threaded take-up spool built into a plastic cartridge. The camera could then be loaded by simply opening the back, dropping in the cartridge and snapping the back shut again. The first Kodak Instamatic for the 126 size cartridge had a single speed shutter and three-element plastic lens. It was synchronised for flashcubes three years later.

But 1963 was famous not only for the first Kodak Instamatic. That year also saw the arrival of the long-awaited Polacolor Land film for instant colour pictures in one minute flat. Like its black and white counterpart, this was a peel-apart process and worked like this:-

The negative material was made up of three subtractive black and white parts, each coated one on top of the other. In each of these parts, there was a differently sensitive silver halide emulsion which reacted to one of the primary colours, and this in turn was linked to a dye developer of the complementary colour (blue-sensitive layer over yellow dye developer, green over magenta, red over cyan). This pack also included barriers to keep the appropriate developer mixing with its own layer and none of the others.

The receiving layer of the Polacolor film was a water-swellable polymer that contained a substance that fixed the dyes and so produced a positive image. There was a built-in self-washing stabilizing system and, after separation from the negative, the finished positive quickly dried with a hard glossy surface.

What is not always appreciated when singing the praises of Polaroid is the fact that the negative section of the early peel-apart Polacolor was made by Kodak and a few years later, in 1969, they were all set to launch their own instant photography cameras. Then came a whisper about a completely new instant colour system from Polaroid known as SX-70 and Kodak scrapped their plans. In the end, they launched their own version of SX-70 in 1977. Of which, more later.

Along with Polacolor in 1963, Polaroid also launched

The Russian made Horizont, together with one of its panoramic pictures.

their first colourpack camera, but its ability to produce instant colour pictures wasn't its only interesting feature. The Polaroid Automatic 100 was the first camera ever made with a transistorized electronic shutter for completely automatic exposure control under all lighting conditions. The shutter was designed, however, not by Polaroid, but by Yashica.

While on the subject of electronic shutters, it is interesting to note that although Polaroid were the first to actually produce a camera with such a shutter, the idea was a

In 1972, there came a new generation of Kodak Instamatics to take 110 size cartridges.

lot older. There was a German patent for an electronic shutter as far back in 1902 which relied on a diaphragm driven by an electric motor controlled by a variable resistor.

In 1934, there was an idea going around for another type that relied on a solenoid to open the blades and incorporated a spring to close them again after the solenoid had been turned off. In 1955 and 1956, both Compur and Prontor took out patents for electronic shutters operated and controlled by photoconductive cells through locks and electronic trigger circuits.

The first commercially available shutters of this type, made in Japan, came in 1963, the year that Polaroid launched the Automatic 100.

Still with Polaroid, the company introduced the Swinger, their first low-priced instant camera, two years later in 1965. But while we are in no way decrying the advantages or wonders of instant photography, it must be admitted that for the serious professional, everything else that year was overshadowed by the arrival of one other long-awaited camera that had been anticipated for years. It was the year of the Leicaflex.

Leica's first single lens reflex was introduced together with four new lenses of the most popular focal lengths and all featuring automatic diaphragms. The Leicaflex sported a newly developed focal plane shutter capable of producing 1/2000 sec and electronic flash synchronisation at 1/100 sec. The viewfinder image was extra bright compared to many of its contemporaries and featured a microprism focusing aid in the centre.

There was another slightly unusual model launched by Canon the next year. This was the Pellix which, to all outward appearances appeared to be a perfectly normal single lens reflex. It was on the inside that things were different. Whereas the conventional single lens reflex employed a mirror which flipped out of the way at the time of exposure, Canon fitted the Pellix with a stationary pellicle prism that split the light from the lens between the film and the viewfinder.

The result was the first ever single lens reflex without the

The first compact single lens reflex was the Olympus OM-1.

usual viewfinder blackout at the moment of exposure. Its only real drawback was the fact that with the light split between viewfinder and film, the viewfinder itself was about one-third darker than a comparable camera and approximately one-third of an f stop less light fell on the film.

The panoramic camera idea was revived again at the 1966 Photokina in the shape of the Russian made Horizont. It took a standard cassette of 35mm film, on which it gave twenty 24 x 58mm frames, each showing a 120 degree angle of view. The lens, which moved horizontally across the camera during exposure somewhat like the old Kodak Panoram of 1899, was an f/2.8 speeded at 1/30, 1/60 and 1/250 sec.

The Kiku (left) was sold in the 1960s as a novelty in souvenir shops. It has already become a collector's item. Will the same thing happen to the Minicam (right), sold as a toy in the 1970s?

By the latter part of the 1960s, automation was becoming more than just a method of helping the photographer to find the correct exposure; more and more, automation itself was actually setting that exposure, freeing the photographer from technicalities and leaving him more time to concentrate on the artistic side of his craft.

The first automatic camera, as we have already seen, was the Super Kodak Six-20 of 1938, but again there had been a patent as far back as 1902 in which a light-measuring system in a camera automatically adjusted the shutter. The Voigtlander Vitomatic, made in 1958, was a fully-automatic camera, but it wasn't until 1968 that the first fully-automatic single lens reflex appeared on the market and, as has been seen before, it was this design that usually set the style for cameras to come.

The first automatic single lens reflex, then, was the Konica Autoreflex T, a shutter priority model with through-the-lens metering. The photographer set the shutter speed between 1 and 1/1000 sec and the camera automatically chose and set the correct aperture. The camera was supplied with a choice of f/1.7, f/1.4 or f/1.2 lenses.

The Konica, of course, still used a mechanical shutter. The Yashica TL Electro-X, produced in 1958, was the first single lens reflex with an electronic shutter but it wasn't until an electronic shutter was linked with automatic exposure in a single lens reflex, that the full potential became obvious. The first camera to combine all three was the Asahi Pentax ES which appeared in 1971. As the first automatic single lens reflex with an electronic shutter, it set a style for a whole new breed of camera.

The Asahi Pentax ES was an aperture priority model

The Polaroid SX-70, instant picture single lens reflex.

122

which meant, of course, that the photographer set the aperture and the camera chose and set its own shutter speed. The shutter was in fact half electronic and half mechanical, the first blind opening mechanically and the second blind being closed electronically after the correct exposure had been given. It was speeded between 1/1000 and a full eight seconds with mechanical speeds between 1/1000 and 1/60 sec. The camera was supplied with a choice of f/1.4, 50mm or f/1.8, 55mm Takumar lenses.

The same year saw the introduction of the Canon F-1; but this was more than just a camera, it was a whole system. Up

The Canon AE-1, first with a
Central Processing Unit, seen
here with Speedlight 155A
and motor drive fitted.

until then, accessories tended to be something which grew
almost willy-nilly; the F-1 system was designed as an entity
— camera, accessories, everything for the complete professional outfit. Right from the start, as many as 10,000
different parts were planned by the Canon company who
saw four main accessories as indispensible for their new

camera: motor drive, automatic exposure control, a booster to make the meter more sensitive and a 250-exposure film chamber.

In 1972, Kodak took their Instamatic design and made it even more portable by reducing the size of the cartridge from 126 to 110. The result was the ultra small Pocket Instamatic cameras which were produced in seven models. Within a very short space of time, most of the other major manufacturers were hot on Kodak's heels, producing 110 cameras of their own. None of the other companies' products could be called Instamatics though. Instamatic is a Kodak trademark and only their cameras should be referred to by that name.

The early 1970s were an interesting time with quite a few surprises in variations on old themes. One such revolutionary idea came from Olympus, who took the concept of the standard 35mm single lens reflex and made it about one-third smaller than any other make. The result was the Olympus OM-1, released at the 1972 Photokina. At that time, the camera was the smallest, lightest, full-frame 35mm single lens reflex in the world, launched as part of a system that featured 280 accessories including thirty-eight interchangeable lenses.

The first instant picture cameras from Kodak. Left to right: EK4, EK6 and EK8.

It took the competition by storm. Some even laughed and said the size would never catch on; photographers, they said, liked something heavier and more 'meaty' in their hands. They didn't laugh for long. Within the next few years, just about every top single lens reflex manufacturer was producing his own compact camera.

By now, electronics were becoming an accepted part of camera manufacture, but in 1972, even they took a new leap forward. The new revolution was a tiny indicator light known as a light emitting diode or LED for short. This device, which is practically everlasting, is in effect a simple diode made of a special semiconductor material such as gallium-arsenide-phosphide which, when attached to a low voltage of around 1.5 volts, lights up with a red or green light.

These LEDs were so small that it became feasible to actually insert them in the camera viewfinder where they could be used to indicate the danger of over or under-exposure, or used in a bank to show the aperture or shutter speed chosen by an automatic system.

The first camera to use LEDs in this way appeared in 1972.

It was the Fujica ST 801, again soon to be followed by other leading manufacturers within the next few years.

'Absolute one-step photography', as Dr. Land called it arrived in 1973 with a completely new instant photography system from Polaroid. It was known simply as SX-70 and, unlike its peel-apart predecessor, it involved no waste paper. With one of the special film packs loaded into the Polaroid SX-70 Land Camera, instant colour pictures were ejected from a slot in the camera's base less than two seconds after the shutter release was pressed. These prints then developed automatically in daylight before your eyes, drying into a hard, flat glossy print 8cm square.

The Polaroid SX-70 Land Camera was a single lens reflex unlike any design ever seen before which used ten-exposure film packs. Inside the pack, apart from the film, there was a wafer-thin battery to power all the camera's functions,

The Polaroid 1000, advertised as 'the world's simplest camera'.

including a motor that drove the reflex mirror and ejected the prints as well as providing power for a flashgun when fitted. With the SX-70, therefore, the photographer didn't have to worry about fitting new batteries. Folded, the camera measured no more than 2.5 x 10 x 18cm.

Computers, very much a thing of the 1970s, finally had their effect on cameras in 1976 with the introduction of the Canon AE-1. The versatility of a modern computer is based mainly on its Central Processing Unit (CPU) and the AE-1, a shutter priority camera, was the first to have one such unit built in. The result was a sophisticated electronic system that enabled the camera to sense and transmit all information to the CPU which in turn controlled the automatic exposure system.

The CPU even controlled flash photography. With the Canon's special Speedlight 155A fitted, the shutter speed was automatically set to 1/60 sec, while the CPU assessed the light from the flashgun in any conditions and automatically set the camera's aperture to the right exposure — all in the brief space of time that it took for the flash to fire.

In 1976, Kodak at last launched their PR-10 instant photography system with the introduction of their EK4 and EK6 instant cameras, working on a similar system to Polaroid's SX-70.

The biggest difference technically between SX-70 and PR-10 film was in the fact that Polaroid used emulsions producing their latent image when the film was exposed to light through the front, while in the Kodak system, light from the lens hit the back of the film and the final result was viewed from the opposite side.

The Throwaway Camera arrived the same year. Made by Rank and used essentially for the premium and promotion industry, this was a 110 camera for sixteen exposures on colour negative film. With a single speed 1/80 sec shutter, fixed f/11 aperture and fixed focus lens, the camera was synchronised for use with Magicube flash and even had a double exposure prevention device.

After the film had been exposed, the whole camera was returned to Rankolor laboratories where it was broken open and the film processed. For the price of the processing, the user then received his sixteen colour prints, complete with a new camera ready loaded with a new film.

The following year, Kodak took their instant system a step forward with the introduction of the EK2 Instant Camera, a simple point and shoot model that left the photographer with little else to do but just that. After

The Throwaway Camera from Rank.

128

The Vivitar 35EF with built-in electronic flash.

exposure, a handle on the EK2's side was turned to eject the developing print.

But at that time, Polaroid were busy launching their own version for SX-70. They called theirs the Polaroid 1000 and advertised it as 'the world's simplest camera'. It was a claim that was well justified because they had improved even on Kodak's simplicity by having the print on theirs ejected automatically. The user quite literally had nothing to do but point the camera, press the shutter release and wait for the developing colour print to be delivered into his hand a second later.

The end of the 1970s saw more and more automation being built into cameras. Electronic flashguns no bigger than an inch square began appearing as standard built-in features on many models such as the Vivitar 35EF released in 1977. This particular model was a full frame 35mm non-reflex camera with automatic exposure control as well as the built-in flash.

The viewfinder showed, besides the scene to be taken, a

flash ready light, aperture scale, bright frame line, parallax correction mask and underexposure warning to tell the user when to switch on the flashgun. All this in a camera that measured only 13.5 x 5.45 x 7.7cm.

One company, Sunpak, famous up until then for their electronic flashguns, even boasted that they had fitted a *camera* in a *flashgun* rather than the other way around.

A camera in a flashgun; the Sunpak SP1000.

It was in the 1970s that stereo photography finally came into its own, though with a system that could never even have been dreamed of back in the days when Wheatstone first approached portrait photographers with his request for stereo pairs. The new system bore little or no resemblance to anything that had gone before. It was called holography and the three-dimensional picture that it produced was called a hologram.

Not that there was anything totally new about the system. A Hungarian scientist named Professor Dennis Gabor first made a hologram in Britain in 1947, using mercury vapour lamps. The result was blurred and dim, but it was three-dimensional.

It was the introduction of lasers in the 1960s and their subsequent application to holography that finally made the hologram a viable proposition, both as an art form and in industry.

So what does a hologram look like? It is a plate that can be viewed without the need for special glasses or any of the viewing apparatus that was needed before for stereo pictures. The viewer simply looks at the plate and sees a three-dimensional picture apparently suspended in mid air. Here, briefly, is how the effect is achieved:-

A laser beam is first split into two separate beams, known as the reference beam and object beam. By means of a lens, the former beam is spread and directed straight onto the photographic plate's emulsion. The second beam is spread and reflected off the object to be photographed and onto the plate. This forms an interference pattern on the emulsion where the two beams meet.

The plate is then developed in a similar way to an ordinary photographic film or plate but instead of normal fixing, the unexposed halide is desensitized and the silver dissolved away by a special bleach. This is to keep grain size down to a minimum. The final result, surprisingly, is a transparent plate that appears to have nothing on it.

But then, when a reconstruction beam is shone from a laser or another source such as mercury vapour lamps, at the same angle as that of the reference beam at the time of taking the hologram, the three-dimensional image appears. This is because the interference pattern on the emulsion is bending, blocking and redirecting the light waves to show an exact copy of the object as it was first recorded.

At this point, the image appears to be hovering *behind* the plate, but by making a second hologram from the original, a true-to-life stereo image of the object appears *in front of* the plate.

In talking about holograms, we are undoubtedly talking about the real future of photography. But there's still a long way to go before a photographer will be able to throw a hologram camera around his neck and show three-dimensional snapshots of his holiday to his friends. Back, then, to the world of more conventional cameras . . .

By 1977, most photographers, amateur and professional alike, had been converted to automatic cameras, and the big discussion of the day was which type of automation was best. In its simplest terms, this could be broken down into two forms: shutter priority (you set the shutter, the camera sets the aperture) or the more popular aperture priority (you set the aperture, the camera sets the shutter speed).

Arguments raged over the merits and/or disadvantages of each system. But when it came right down to it, most agreed there was something to be said on each side. After all, if you were photographing sport or something similar that demanded a certain shutter speed, you needed shutter priority; if you were working on a subject where depth of field was more important than the speed of the shutter, then you needed aperture priority.

What everyone agreed on was that the ideal solution would be a camera that gave the choice of both. But such a thing didn't exist. Not until late 1977 anyway.

The first camera in the world to offer a straight choice between aperture priority, shutter priority or complete manual override was the Minolta XD-7, released in the Autumn of 1977 and available to the general public by early 1978.

The Minolta XD-7 used a simple three-position switch to select whichever mode the photographer needed for the job in hand. All information such as shutter and aperture chosen was displayed in the viewfinder and focusing was helped by microprism and split-image aids.

Along with the XD-7, Minolta also released a motor wind and a remarkable new flashgun known as the Auto Electro-flash 200X. The two went well together because the flash-gun was capable of keeping pace with the motor wind's two-

The Minolta XD-7, first camera with a choice of shutter or aperture priority.

The Konica C35AF, the first really viable auto-focus camera.

frames-per-second running time.

Only one thing was now left for the photographer to operate manually, namely the focusing; and that was finally automated in the Spring of 1978.

The camera was the Konica C35AF, an automatic compact non-reflex model with built-in electronic flash, a 38mm f/2.8 lens and programmed shutter speeded at 1/60, 1/25 and 1/250 sec. The auto-focusing mechanism worked by way of two windows. A computer control within the camera compared the images from these two viewpoints, used the information to calculate the distance and set the lens accordingly, together with the right exposure — all in the time it took the photographer to press the shutter release.

At the beginning of this short history, I mentioned that the difficulty was knowing where to start. Now that I have come this far, the difficulty is knowing where to finish. At the time of writing — early in 1978 — the Minolta XD-7 and the Konica C35AF represent the latest instalment in the history of the camera. What can possibly come next?

Well, undoubtedly other manufacturers will soon follow Minolta's lead in choice of shutter or aperture priority. And it's a fair bet that the near future will see an auto-focus single lens reflex with built-in electronic flash and motor drive.

Yet looked at objectively, it almost seems that we've gone about as far as we can go. Holography, electronics, LEDs in viewfinders, throwaway cameras, automation of the most sophisticated kind — what will the makers dream up next?

As to that, only time will tell . . .

Acknowledgements

For every book of this type, there is usually someone without whom, the author says, the book would never have been written. In this case, I am indebted to Dr. Robert White who, at the time of writing, is Chairman of the Museum Working Party at the Royal Photographic Society. It was as a result of a lecture by Dr. White some years ago that I first became interested in vintage cameras and subsequently started collecting. Without that interest, this book would never have been written.

Since the night of that lecture, Bob White has become not only a friend, but also a guide and valuable source of information on all things photographically antique. My thanks then to Bob for access to his private collection of cameras, his library and — most of all — to the inner workings of his mind.

Thanks also to Brian Coe of the Kodak Museum, together with all the press and public relations people whose various departments deal with Asahi Pentax, Canon, Kodak, Konica, Leica, Minolta, Nikon, Rank, Rollei, Technical and Optical and Topcon.

Without whom . . .

Picture credits

The numbers following each credit refer to the pages on which the pictures appear. Where more than one illustration appears on a page, the appropriate photograph is identified in brackets.

Crown Copyright. Science Museum, London: 15, 21, 22, 24, 33 (first picture on glass), 36-37, 46 (Meagher camera), 52, 54.
Photo. Science Museum, London: 9, 14, 19, 23, 27, 28-29, 59 (photograph), 60, 78.
Lent to the Science Museum, London by Johnson's of Hendon Ltd: 20.
Photo. Science Museum, London, by courtesy of the Royal Photographic Society: 12, 34, 35.
The Kodak Museum: 51, 53, 57, 59 (camera), 64, 70-71, 81 (Debrie Sept), 92 (Retina), 102 (Super Kodak Six-20), 116, 120.
Gernsheim Collection, Humanities Research Centre, The University of Texas at Austin: 10-11.
Royal Scottish Museum: 26.

With the exception of product pictures kindly supplied by the camera companies concerned, all other pictures in this book are the copyright of John Wade, Terry Scott or Dr. Robert White.

Index